SERIOUSWORK

Self published by

ProMeet, an independent imprint.

Edition

First published in November 2016, this 4rd edition edition has been revised with new typesetting, better proof reading and a new preface. Edition 4 is self published via KDP

Disclaimer

Although the authors have made every effort to ensure that the information in this book was correct at the time of going to print, the authors do not assume and hereby disclaim any liability to any party for any loss, damage, or disruption caused by errors or omissions, whether such errors or omissions result from negligence, accident, or any other cause

ISBN Print: 9798502569989

Connect

▸ @SeriousWrk
✉ Sean@Serious.Global

SERIOUSWORK

HOW TO FACILITATE MEETINGS & WORKSHOPS
USING THE LEGO® SERIOUS PLAY® METHOD

with conscious incompetence

Written, & designed by
SEAN BLAIR
MARKO RILLO

With help from
OUR PARTNERS

Production: SEAN BLAIR
Publisher: PROMEET

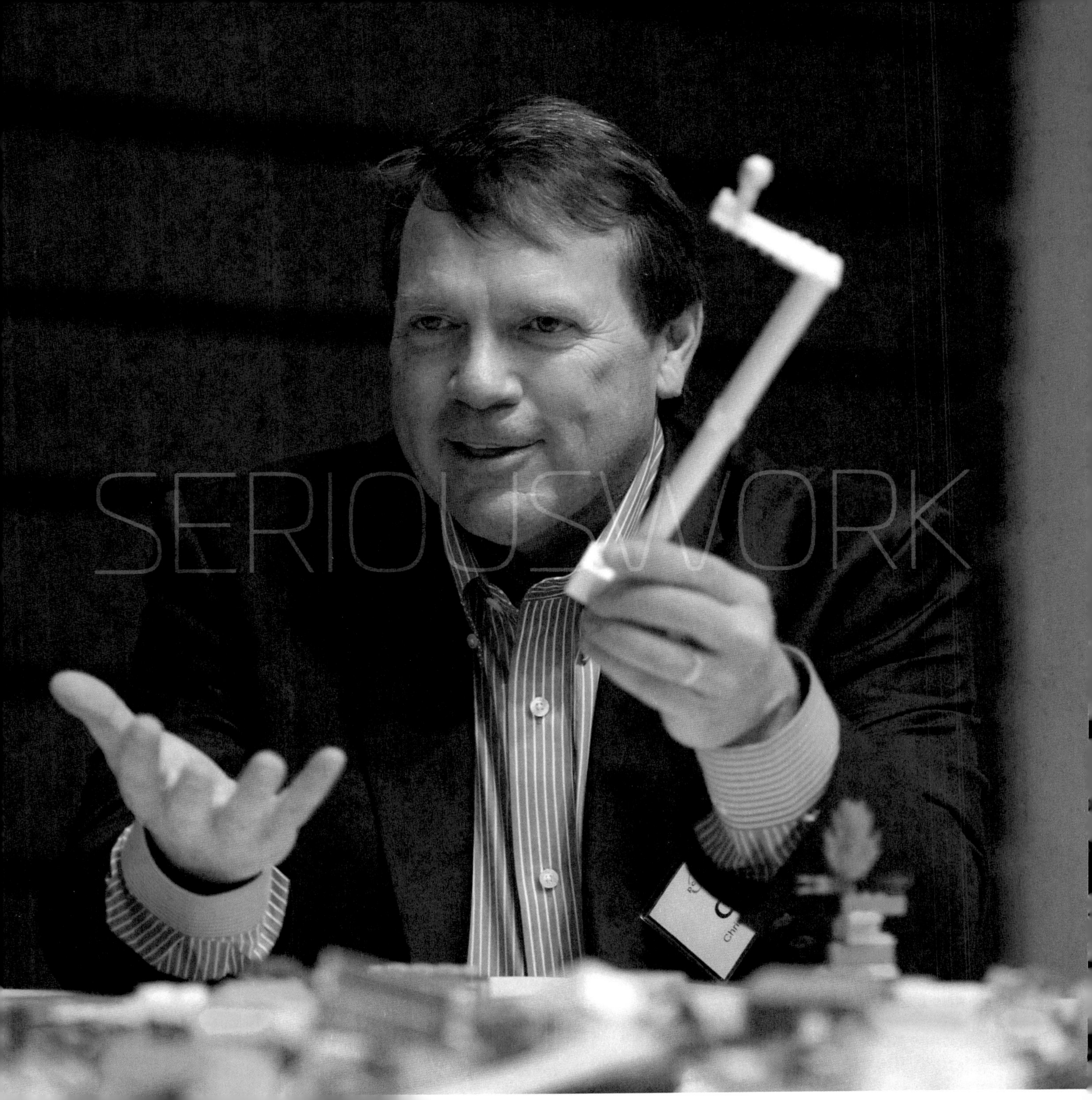
SERIOUS WORK

Contents

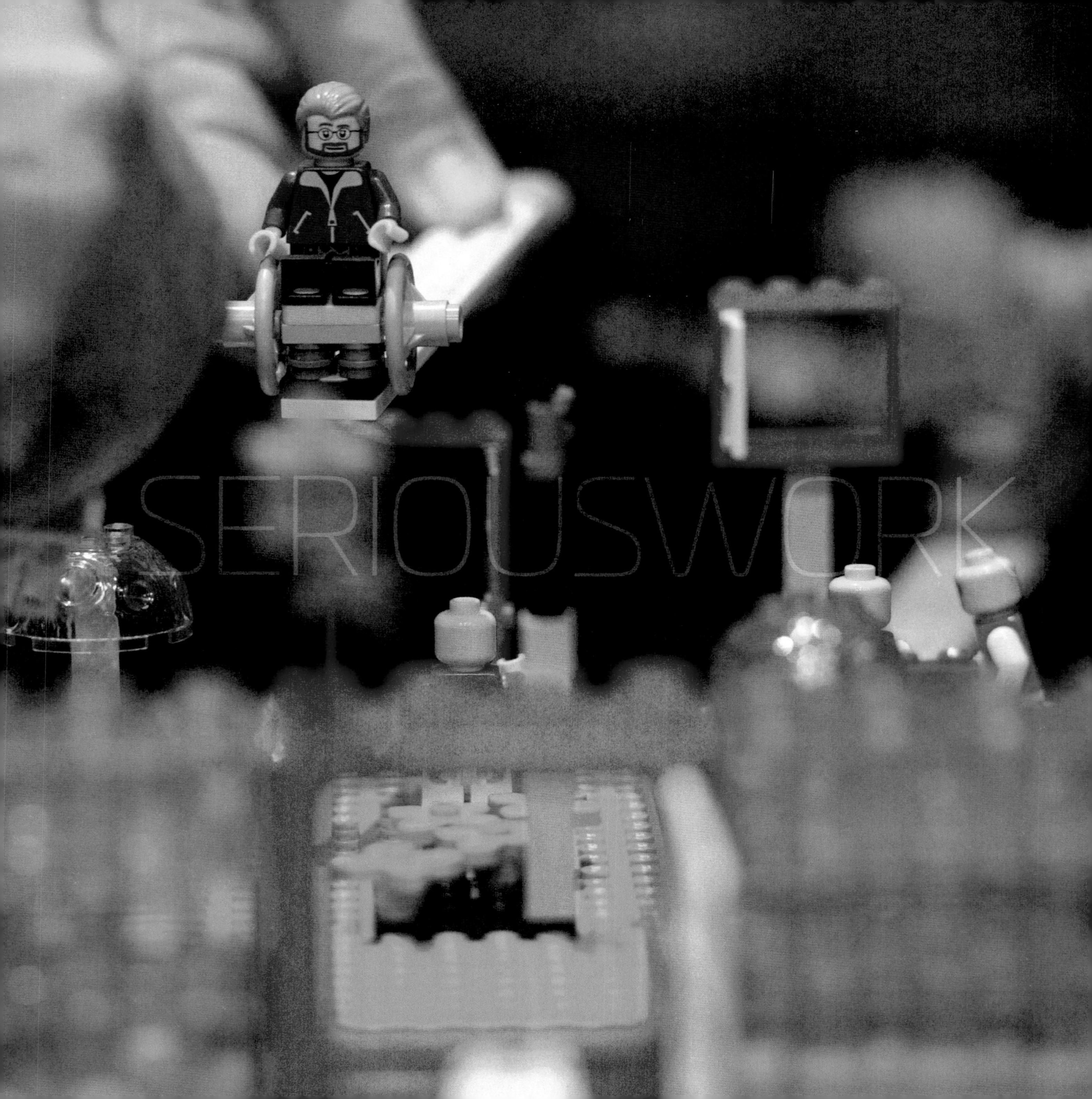
SERIOUSWORK

Partners

SeriousWork is co-authored by nine partners who wrote Part 6 of this book.

Camilla Nørgaard Jensen
USA/Denmark

Dieter Reuther
USA

Kristina Nyzell
Sweden

Mercedes Hoss
Germany

Kim Pong Lim
Singapore

Patrizia Bertini
Italy

Eli de Friend
Switzerland

Maria Stashenko
Russia

Oliver Knapman
China

Foreword

A message from the future

It was an unlikely tale. LEGO - the company who saved the World! Really, it was that awesome!

No one predicted it, no one saw it, not even the people who pioneered the method. And no one could have been more surprised than the executives who ran this toy company. By early 2018 they had mastered selling LEGO® theme kits to children all over the world. That's what LEGO was famous for.

But then a decision made at the LEGO Group some 20 years earlier started to have unexpected and positive consequences.

The insane idea that Johan Roos and Bart Victor had in 1996 began to help people see, communicate and understand in new ways.

Hundreds of thousands of people started using LEGO® Serious Play®. A combination of LEGO Serious Play with the wisdom of higher level human-to-human communication processes, and insights unlocked through advances in brain science was powerful.

People finally had purposeful conversations. Leaders engaged their teams in a truly participatory way. Everybody started telling stories that had deeper meaning. They could reflect deeper thoughts and beliefs. They used colourful metaphors to engage emotionally.

They started understanding consequences of their aspirations. They became able to see and understand systems.

As LEGO Serious Play became a widely used and legitimate tool, more people could explore purpose, vision and plans systemically.

And the models spoke back, not literally of course, but people were wholly able to explore the full pictures of each other's perspective and how they influenced each other.

Models of interconnected systems showed consequences that had been impossible to observe before. This enabled human to human and heart to heart exchange on root causes.

Intangible ideas, attitudes, influences and beliefs took form in LEGO® models and became part of the language and method of cutting edge of modern planning.

LEGO Serious Play became as common as marker pens and flipcharts. Bricks were found at offices of executives and leaders, coaches and consultants, teachers and trainers, administrators and policy makers, researchers and scientists, therapists and thinkers, innovators and engineers. Everybody who needed to think-together had them.

The early pioneers of '96 created LEGO Serious Play. The group that followed developed it. Then it was made Open Source and a new wave of thousands of practitioners took it to a whole new level.

Who saw that one coming?

Preface from the original edition

2016. LEGO® Serious Play® is thriving.

How is it that a child's toy has become a serious strategy tool used by some of the world's best known organisations? And what might be the relevance of this method in your work?

This practical book is intended for people who run meetings: leaders, managers, facilitators and coaches, who are seeking ways to help teams work-together well.

A very brief history of LEGO Serious Play

The serious play story began in 1996 when Institute for Management Development (IMD) professors Johan Roos and Bart Victor created the "serious play" concept and process as a way to enable managers to describe, create and challenge their views of their business. LEGO joined the story during an IMD program for the top 300 leaders in the LEGO® Company.

Roos and Victor presented their early ideas in a short article published by IMD in 1998 entitled "In Search for Original Strategies: How About Some Serious Play?"

Presented with the findings of the work at IMD, LEGO® CEO Kjeld Kirk Kristiansen sponsored a company under the auspices of LEGO® called Executive Discovery.

Bart Victor led the product development and commercialization process of Serious Play at Executive Discovery.

He invited staff from LEGO® and Professor Dave Owens from Vanderbilt University to help bring the first product to market. The first LEGO Serious Play 'application' was called Real-Time Strategy.

LEGO Serious Play was developed into a consulting method used by companies including Daimler Chrysler, Roche, SABMiller, Tupperware, Nokia and Orange.

At the same time, Johan Roos and Kjeld Kirk Kristiansen established the research effort at the aptly named 'Imagination Lab', a Swiss think tank that between 2001-2006 produced 74 research papers, many journal articles and 4 books.

The result of 15 years development? A powerful method to solve problems, explore ideas and achieve objectives based on management theory[1] using a toy.

In 2010 LEGO® made the method open source. This decision created a community of practice and today, unleashed, we find the method thriving in a wide range of applications.

---

[1] Constructivism (Piaget 1951). Constructionism (Harel & Papert 1991). Complex adaptive system theory (Holland 1995). Autopoietic corporate epistemology (von Krogh & Roos 1994; 1995)

The book aims to help you understand what LEGO® Serious Play® is and how it works.

We hope it helps you journey towards unconscious competence in using LEGO Serious Play.

Our purpose in writing.

To help further legitimise a brilliant and powerful method.

Preface to the 2020 edition

We first published SERIOUSWORK in November 2016 and this update follows, nearly four years later. The main change to this version, published in October 2020, is better typography.

Let us explain. In 2018 we were approached by a lovely chap called Jens Dröge. Jens asked if he could translate the book into German. We agreed and he spent many hours working on the translation.

We were also approached by a wonderful man, Dennis Brunotte who offered to publish SERIOUSWORK in German with a respected publisher called Vahlen.

In the process that followed the book was edited and re-typeset, and in 2019 'SERIOUSWORK MEETINGS UND WORKSHOPS MIT DER LEGO® SERIOUS PLAY®- METHODE MODERIEREN' was published.

The quality of the typesetting was so much better in the German version, having been refined by a professional book designer, Frau Deuringer.

The original English version was not as well proof read as it should have been and both typographical errors and the typesetting came in for mild and fair criticism in book reviews on Amazon.

Good design is one of our four guiding principles so we had long intended to update the book when time allowed and some years later, here we are.

LEGO Serious Play was made 'Open Source' in 2010, (see pg 64) so the last four years, since the method became accessible to all, also represents nearly half the lifetime of publicly driven innovation of the method itself.

And in these years we have made three significant developments.

Firstly, world class training

After we published SERIOUSWORK in 2016, we asked, *'Is there a better way to teach the method?'*

SeriousWork trainees practising the facilitation skills we teach.

Let's wind the clock back and set the scene.

After it was invented in the late 1990's, the only place you could learn the method was by being trained at and by the LEGO® Group.

In 2010 the LEGO® Group made LEGO Serious Play open source. After that, the LEGO® Group offered no training of any kind in the method. If you wanted to take a class to learn to facilitate LEGO Serious Play you had two main options. You could learn with TAMT or SP[1], both of whom had folks who had worked at the LEGO® Group.

Therefore by the time SERIOUSWORK was published, almost all LEGO Serious Play training was based on the original training model that the LEGO® Group created. This model was based on a master/learner ethos and used a '7 application techniques' process framework.

Our own experience of being taught this way, and subsequent practice in the field, showed three main weaknesses of this model.

Firstly the transition from classroom, to front of room was a problem. Students simply did not practise facilitation skills in a four day training led by a 'master'. The unintended consequence of this style of teaching is that most learnt to be participants not facilitators, and subsequently left trainings with low confidence (including the authors!).

Secondly the subject focus was LEGO Serious Play (a rigid definition), rather than a focus on the

facilitation of the method, and some of the underlying models did not make sense to us and others.

Lastly, the original model for teaching the method, strongly informed by its academic fathers[2] deep interest in strategy, meant that all students were taught 'systems applications' (such as Real Time Strategy) that ultimately most would never use.

Having learnt about these limitations, in 2017 we set out with a blank sheet of paper, and it has to be said, by 'standing on the shoulders of giants' to ask, *'Is there a better way to teach the method?'*

We designed a very different approach and began training in 2017.

Our training is *practise based*, meaning trainees practise facilitating during training, it is *facilitation focused*, combining LEGO Serious Play with other brilliant facilitation tools, and is delivered in 1, 2, 3 or 4 day trainings, *depending upon what people want to do after training.*

The feedback we have received from people trained by both schools is that this new training model is the gold standard. Authors make claims about their own offers, so don't take our word for it, read the many reviews on LinkedIn of Sean Blair - our chief learning designer!

We now have training associates in Germany (Jens Dröge), North America (Mia Eng), South America (Héctor Villarreal), Scandinavia and Italy (Mirjami Sipponen-Damonte) and soon to be in China…

[1] TAMT: The Association of Master Trainers. SP: Strategic Play

[2] Institute for Management Development (IMD) professors Johan Roos and Bart Victor

New techniques (and two new books)

In March 2020 we published 'MASTERING THE LEGO SERIOUS PLAY METHOD: 44 Techniques for trained LEGO Serious Play Facilitators'.

Our second book has a focus on shared model building, something SERIOUSWORK explicitly did not set out to explain. So MASTERING was both an update to the facilitation techniques and the logical second in the series. Ironically, MASTERING, launched just as COVID-19 hit Europe, had a singular focus on face-to-face facilitation.

In updating the book you are holding in your hands, we needed to decide whether to do a big rewrite, to include all the new techniques we had learnt, or whether to leave it true to the original. COVID-19 made that decision for us. Use these crazy times to write a new book.

Online LEGO Serious Play

So, depending upon where in the world you live, somewhere between January and March 2020 your world must have changed.

If you had asked us before COVID-19 could you run a LEGO Serious Play workshop (or train others how to facilitate) online our answer would have been 'no-way'.

Necessity really is the mother of invention, so in March 2020 when we realised COVID-19 would have a profound impact on face-to-face LEGO Serious Play we set to work. Our aim was to create new techniques that would build upon the fundamental principles of the method, and solve problems about how to facilitate shared model building online.

As you can see from the photo opposite, we worked out how to run LEGO Serious Play just as effectively online as face-to-face, and our new book, 'HOW TO FACILITATE THE LEGO® SERIOUS PLAY® METHOD ONLINE, New Facilitation Techniques for Shared Models and #Covidsafe Face-To-Face' is now available.

We also train novice and experienced LEGO Serious Play facilitators these new online techniques in one and two day online trainings, https://www.serious. global/learn/online-lego-serious-play-facilitator-training/

Certified / Accredited Professional Facilitator

Our final big project in the last few years has been to develop a competency based assessment to award experienced facilitators a stand-out-from-the-crowd-certificate that proves a professional level of competency in designing & delivering workshops.

At the time of going to press with this update of SERIOUSWORK, we have prototyped and successfully tested this accreditation process.

We are seeking a neutral body to adopt the administration and awarding of such a certificate, as we think this should not be related to any one specific training provider.

Four years provides much learning

So now you're more or less up to date on the bigger developments since our first book. We have learnt a huge amount about LEGO Serious Play, and if anything we see more untapped potential in the method now than we did four years ago.

The LEGO Serious Play community is gathering in new and non-partisan forms. The unaffiliated LSPConnect forum welcomes facilitators, trained or untrained to meet, share in the spirit of generosity and learn together. The feeling in this community is one of optimism and opportunity, you would be welcome too. Find out more at https://www. lspconnect.events/

Begin here

SERIOUSWORK was our first 'beginners book' and has sold all over the world in English, German and Spanish. It's a great place to start your LEGO Serious Play journey, we hope you find it a useful resource to get you going.

Sean Blair - October 2020

See all these new developments at **www.serious.global**

Authors

 Sean Blair

https://uk.linkedin.com/in/sean-blair

Sean is the founder of ProMeet, an international professional facilitation business. He facilitates learning, growth and change in meetings, workshops, conferences, including with LEGO® Serious Play® all over the world.

Sean is one of the LEGO Serious Play community's most active practitioners. He set up the first LEGO Serious Play MeetUp group in London. There are now over 40 LEGO Serious Play MeetUp groups globally.

Described as a systems innovator and 'itinerant provocateur', he imagines a better world. Unwittingly this annoys traditionalists.

Sean is part of the leadership team of EMENA International Association of Facilitators (IAF), an organisation that promotes the power of facilitation. He is an IAF Certified™ Professional Facilitator and a winner of an IAF 'Facilitation Impact Award'.

Marko Rillo

https://www.linkedin.com/in/markorillo

Marko's passion for and early adoption of LEGO Serious Play led him to establish the SeriousPlayPro community website that now has over 2000 members.

Marko first heard about LEGO Serious Play at a conference with Serious Play guru Professor Johan Roos in 2005 and began experimenting with the method.

In 2007 he started his doctoral studies at the University of St. Gallen in Switzerland where a former Imagination Lab research fellow professor Claus D. Jacobs became one of his academic mentors.

Marko participated in one of the last LEGO Serious Play certification training sessions that was provided directly under the auspices of the LEGO® Corporation. He has facilitated at tiny start-ups and international multinationals, he has also helped create a vision for Estonia!

The brief story of this book

Sean first found Marko virtually via the SeriousPlayPro website when he asked for advice in running his first large LEGO Serious Play workshop for 320 people.

We met in person in 2015 at a LEGO Serious Play facilitators conference in Billund and discussed the lack of writing about LEGO Serious Play.

We had both been thinking about how to legitimise LEGO Serious Play and help it become a more widely accepted and used tool.

Despite there being an excellent Open Source Guide, and a good book on the history, territory and theory of LEGO Serious Play, there was no book that explained the LEGO Serious Play process.

So we agreed to write **SERIOUSWORK**, a how-to book with supporting resources to help people understand the LEGO Serious Play basics.

To use LEGO Serious Play on important assignments we firmly recommend using a trained facilitator or attending a training programme first!

We imagine readers might use this book as a step before training, or as a guide to try the basics with Build Level 1: Individual Model building in low risk workshops.

We hope this book helps you begin to discover the incredible power of LEGO Serious Play.

Acknowledgements

Isaac Newton famously once said, *'If I have seen further, it is by standing on the shoulders of giants'*, we are not claiming to see much further, but we can only produce this book, thanks to those brilliant people who invented and developed this method.

We would like to acknowledge and thank all who created and championed LEGO® Serious Play® for making this book possible.

We acknowledge and thank our teachers Robert Rasmussen, Per Kristiansen and Jacqueline Lloyd Smith. They taught us LEGO Serious Play and have our respect for being the early pioneers of teaching the method.

We have both had the privilege to talk to hundreds of LEGO Serious Play facilitators - creative individuals and members of the global Serious Play Pro community. The discussions over the years have provided us with many opportunities to learn. Thank you to everyone who has posted questions, case studies and comments.

LEGO® Foundation

When we had the idea for this book, the first person we contacted was Jette Orduna at the LEGO® Foundation. We are grateful to her and the LEGO® Foundation for giving us permission to write this book.

We also want to say thank you to the following people and organisations for help in the creation of the book:

Thanks to our generous case study clients

The core part of this book is part 5. This is where we use real life examples to help you understand the practical aspects of facilitating LEGO Serious Play meetings and workshops.

This book would not be possible without the generosity of our case study clients in allowing us to share the stories and photos of LEGO Serious Play. A big thanks to:

Especially: Karl Anton and the IPTV team from Telia Telco. Peter Brenner, Edward Bignold and the team at IGH. Jim Bowes and the Manifesto Digital team. Rita Fevereiro and the team at FutureLearn.

Customers

We thank all our customers. The biggest learning for any facilitator happens at meetings. We are enormously grateful for the faith you have put in us at every LEGO Serious Play meeting and workshop you have allowed us to facilitate

Photos

During many workshops over the years we took photos during meetings and workshops to record what happened for our clients.

When we took them, we did not imagine writing a book, yet LEGO® is such a visual tool and we are grateful to be able to produce a book with colourful photos of people doing **serious work** with LEGO® at our workshops.

Thanks especially to Julien Carlier, Mieke Barbé, Agnieszka Ziemiańska, David Lardier, Karin Krogh, Thomas Vig, Hans Ravnkjær Larsen, Valérie Guillet, Anette Palm, Janet Skorepa, Deborah Sexton, Richard Tyrie, Federico Toja, Serge Radovcic, Axel Pawlik, Jochem de Ruig, Kaveh Ranjbar, Paul Rendek, Andrew de la Haye, Dr Marianne Guldbrandsen, Milad Ahmed, Richard Ball, Christina Lindeberg, David Dawson, James O'Halloran, Louise Prideaux, Linda Drew, Karen Brown, Elizabeth Rouse, Lawrence Zeegen, Laura Gander-Howe, Anna-Liisa Reinson, Inga Keldo, Kaspar Kalve and Justin Buck.

We are grateful to the LEGO® artist Sean Kenney for allowing us to reproduce a photo of one of his LEGO® Polar Bear sculptures. Thanks also to Michi Yahata from Sean's studio.

Helpers, testers and proof readers

We are fortunate to have help proof reading and testing the ideas in this book. The book is considerably better thanks to Caroline Jessop, Paul Brown, Tammy Seibert, Kersti Peenema, Madis Talmar and Helen Batt. Thank you.

Partners who contributed to the book

We are very grateful to have partners who have shared their experience, advice, stories and insight. This book is very much the better with your brilliant contributions. Thanks for believing in us. Let's create the future of LEGO Serious Play together!

Production advice and help

Thanks to Dan Start for his excellent publishing advice and in the 2020 edition to Dennis Brunotte for helping improve the typography.

Introduction

The objective of this book is to enable you to understand how to facilitate LEGO® Serious Play® based meetings and workshops.

It is a practical 'how to' book, that has case studies, step-by-step guides and templates from common build level one applications that you can adapt to your own needs.

It is intended for leaders, managers, facilitators, coaches and business development professionals who are seeking ways to help teams work well together.

To become an effective and professional facilitator of LEGO Serious Play, requires learning by doing, attending a training programme is the only way to master the skills shown in this book.

But our hope is this book gives you enough knowledge to learn about or try basic LEGO Serious Play techniques: to facilitate goal setting, ideas workshops, and explore team life through vision, values and behaviours workshops.

We live in a complex and challenging time where technological, environmental, social and political change demand that we better understand system consequences of our decisions.

In writing this book, we also had a greater purpose: **To help legitimise a brilliant and powerful method.**

LEGO Serious Play Three Build Levels

BUILD LEVEL 3
System models

BUILD LEVEL 2
Shared models

BUILD LEVEL 1
Individual models

This book's **primary** focus is Build **Level 1: Individual Model Building.**

MANIFESTO GUIDING PRINCIPLE

HELP PEOPLE TO SEE SOMETHING
DIFFERENT

MANIFESTO VALUES

COLLABORATE
TO CREATE GREAT WORK

Models of a 'Simple Guiding Principle' and a value created at a workshop for the London digital agency "Manifesto.".

Workshop outputs like these created by participants bring ideas to life. **See Part 5.5 to read about and see the process that resulted in these models.**

It therefore seems paradoxical that LEGO® bricks, a product conceived as a children's toy, can enable teams to communicate more powerfully and explore complex organisational issues and unintended consequences especially at build level three.

Legitimise LEGO Serious Play

In buying this book and using LEGO Serious Play to understand your work challenges you're also helping legitimise a process tool kit you'll wish you'd known about years ago. Thank you for joining our quest.

LEGO Serious Play in brief

LEGO Serious Play was first created in the mid-1990's by Professors Johan Roos and Bart Victor 'as a way to enable managers to describe, create and challenge their views of their business'.

Today, the LEGO Serious Play method has been used all over the world by organisations including:

Airbus, Fujitsu, Toyota, Coca-Cola, Fedex, Google, MasterCard, Microsoft, NASA, Nissan, Pfizer, Proctor & Gamble, Target, Telia Telco, Unilever, Waitrose and the World Bank Group; reputable universities including Harvard, MIT, Cambridge, IMD and Oxford; International organisations, including the EU, UNESCO, UNDP; Government ministries and agencies in: Denmark, Estonia, Turkey and United Kingdom, to name a few!

What is LEGO Serious Play?

If you ask different people what LEGO Serious Play is you might well get different answers. The reason? Because it's many things in the same package.

LEGO Serious Play is a Method

It is a systematic method that enables people to use LEGO® bricks to solve problems, explore ideas and achieve objectives.

LEGO Serious Play is a Process

It is a structured process where participants proceed through a series of steps to think, build, tell a story, reflect and refine, to develop a shared understanding of the issue at hand.

LEGO Serious Play is a Communication tool or language

LEGO Serious Play enables three modes of communication: visual, auditory and kinaesthetic. The models enable enhanced expression, deeper listening and better memory.

Shared model building allows teams to understand each others' interpretation and create deeper shared meaning of key ideas.

LEGO Serious Play is a Service

It is a service provided by trained facilitators, trainers or coaches who use LEGO® bricks hand in hand with other material tools to help individuals or teams achieve objectives and create outcomes.

LEGO Serious Play is a Framework

As a framework or philosophy LEGO Serious Play is a participatory mode of leadership that is democratic, all-inclusive, playful, goal-driven and constructive.

LEGO Serious Play is a Product line

It is also a patented and trademarked product line of LEGO® corporation. LEGO® and its subsidiary Executive Discovery, patented LEGO Serious Play in early 2001 as "a program, method and materials for enhancing creative thinking, communication, decision-making and strategic planning." (U.S. Patent no. 20020103774-A1).

LEGO Serious Play is a Meeting tool

While some applications might need a five day workshop, we also have witnessed its power to activate people in small and large groups, in brief interventions of just 10 minutes to a workshop over several days.

LEGO Serious Play – a process to enhance innovation and performance.

Based on research which shows that this kind of 'hands-on, minds-on' learning produces a deeper, more meaningful understanding of the world and its possibilities, the LEGO Serious Play methodology deepens the reflection process and enables effective communication, for everyone in your organisation.

The process of making something, which is then discussed, leads to more valuable, more insightful and more honest discussions.

The creative process of making something prompts the brain to work in a different way, unlocking new perspectives.

When participants construct an object to represent what they think is important about the issue at hand, before discussion, the downsides of positional power are removed and this allows people to focus on the ideas, not the personalities.

This is not like the typical discussions that occur at work, where a dominant personality identifies the 'key issues' at the start, and then the rest of the conversation follows from there.

In LEGO Serious Play, everyone builds, and everyone shares, resulting in more democratic meetings, enabling equal 'air time' from all participants.

Indeed, the process of building and collaborating often produces insights which simply would not have appeared in regular discussions.

When we give shape and form to our imagination, by constructing and externalizing concepts we make our ideas tangible and shareable.

This helps us reflect better on our own ideas, as well as enabling others to reflect with us.

To make an analogy, LEGO Serious Play is a bit like making 3D prints of your own thoughts.

The models allow others to see your thoughts and ask questions about them.

LEGO Serious Play creates an engaging hands-on environment, where the activity is perceived as meaningful, one's abilities are in balance with the challenge at hand, and one has the tools to express and communicate emerging knowledge.

The organisation and scope of the book

As a 'how to' book, we don't cover the history of LEGO Serious Play or the theoretical and scientific ideas that underpin LEGO Serious Play[2].

In part 1, the facilitative mindset of the participatory leader:

We introduce the idea of participatory leadership as an enlightened and effective mode of leadership that today's times require.

Adopt the idea that facilitation is a mindset of a participatory leadership, to enable yourself to lead clever people working on complex challenges.

Because participatory leaders use time working together to get the very best out of participants, this inevitably suggests they have a facilitative mindset.

This is an important idea that supports the LEGO Serious Play method which likewise values input from every person, encourages diverse and creative thinking and allows participants to understand ideas systemically.

We hope you'll see that despite its name, LEGO Serious Play, is more than just a fad cheered for by a bunch of LEGO® enthusiasts, but a way to be a participatory leader.

Next we cover 'facilitation fundamentals' and signpost you to the core competency framework promoted by the International Association of Facilitators.

In part 2 we cover the vital step in planning any meeting or workshop: objective setting.

Getting clear on the outcomes and objectives for your meeting.

This may sound obvious, but as professional facilitators, this is the stage where we often add real value, and it's the stage that determines much of the process to be used in meetings. Because objectives trump agendas, we hope you might never use a traditional agenda again, and instead use objectives to drive meetings.

In part 3 we introduce you to the core LEGO Serious Play ideas and etiquette that underpin all meetings and workshops.

---

[2] See 'Building Better Business Using The LEGO Serious Play method' by Rasmussen & Kristiansen.

Then we talk about bricks and offer you ideas about where and how to get them, as well as give you ideas about what kind of volume and what sort you might need, to get the best out of participants in different kinds of workshops.

In part 4 we show you how to give your workshop participants the three basic LEGO Serious Play skills.

We describe how to give workshop participants technical building skills, use of metaphors and storytelling skills using LEGO® models.

Then we'll show you how to help participants share and listen better than in traditional meetings.

These skills will free your meeting participants up from concerns or worries about not having used LEGO® before (or for many years) and enable them to express ideas, concepts, feelings, facts, reflections and insights powerfully using just a few bricks.

Part 5 takes you through five common workshop applications.

In each we offer you a sample workshop plan, taken from a real past project. We give you detailed facilitation instructions about how we prepared, ran and followed up from the workshops.

We offer you these case studies so you can see how these ideas were applied in practice and what outputs and outcomes were created. You can download and adapt our templates for your own use.

In Part 6 our partners share stories, advice and experience from running hundreds of LEGO Serious Play workshops.

Then we offer you ideas about how to manage time, mistakes to watch for and how to make LEGO® Serious Movies.

In part 7 we offer you ideas about how to become a virtuoso practitioner and explain why reading a book will make you consciously incompetent.

We set out three ways you can develop your skills and signpost you to a growing community of LEGO Serious Play facilitators.

We think the book makes most sense if read in the order outlined, there are some concepts introduced in earlier chapters that are referenced in later chapters.

Part 1

The facilitative mindset of participatory leaders

The facilitative mindset of participatory leaders

PARTICIPATORY LEADERSHIP - A LEADERSHIP PARADIGM FOR A COMPLEX WORLD

The participatory leadership paradigm is based on **respect** and **engagement**. It **constructively focuses energy** in every human to human encounter.

A more advanced, more democratic and more effective model of leadership, it **harnesses diversity, builds community**, and **creates shared responsibility for action**.

It deepens individual and collective **learning** yielding real **development and growth**.

Participatory Leadership

This chapter:

Advocates that participatory leadership is a smart way to lead clever people in a complex world

Suggests that a facilitative mindset is the way of a participative leader

Proposes that LEGO® Serious Play® is one way that participatory leaders can facilitate teams to think and work together

Don't participate?!

What is the point of having a meeting where people do not, or are not 'allowed' to, participate?

Many professional people have experienced 'meeting agony', where what people really think is not welcome or where 20% of the people do 80% of the talking.

Have you been there? You know what we're saying?

Let's be honest, if you have ever encountered a meeting where your participation was not welcomed (or facilitated) it wasn't because you didn't have a contribution to make, but because

your contribution was just not that important in the mind of the meeting leader.

You could say they weren't a participatory leader.

Participate

A better way. Participatory leadership is a smart way to lead clever people in complex times of unprecedented and accelerating change.

The pace of change has sky-rocketed in the last decade and is set to accelerate further. Change driven by technological innovation, the growth and changing nature of globalisation, environmental pressures and the changing social expectations and attitudes, towards politics, society and culture.

This means that no single leader or manager alone is able to resolve all the issues that their organisations face. They need to engage their teams and involve people and partners, inside and outside their organisations.

In other words, they need to facilitate the participation of teams of bright people in service of meaningful and shared objectives.

However, there is a participation problem that is all too frequent in contemporary leadership culture. Whilst some leaders might say they welcome honest discussion, a real, and often unconscious,

'action strategy'[3] instead seeks control and protection: fear of losing control or looking silly.

Management academics Argyris and Schön[4] suggest that while the leaders verbal 'espoused theory', says they want to engage others, their actual actions or 'theory in use' attempts to 'control and protect'.

So on one hand, contemporary leaders are often expected to be clear, powerful and decisive. On the other hand, because of complexities of today's world, they need to involve many people and have honest discussion about unknowns.

Some leaders struggle to combine these two paradoxical aims well, and some cultures value or nurture 'over confidence' and the appearance of control, over a wiser and more democratic path of joint enquiry and true participation.

Meeting agony: A leader gathers a meeting. A few people talk a lot. Some daydream about more pressing matters.

Some have their noses deep in their mobile devices.

Occasional interaction between the few occurs, but the ratio between active and passive participants is heavily tilted towards the latter. No one is really listening, seeking to understand others' perspectives or views.

There are good reasons why organisation researchers have labelled meetings as the gravest source of inefficiency in teams today.

Most of us have received no formal training on how to run or participate in a meeting. Often meeting objectives are unclear and sometimes the participants might not suit the aims of the meeting. Frequently 'rules of behaviour' are left to individual interpretation at worst, toxic or punitive cultures bring out the worst in people.

Meeting process is often unclear, with 'discussion' the default (and very poor) mode of exchange. Ladies and gentlemen, this is meeting agony, and sadly most of us have experienced it. This can be avoided by using the principles of participatory leadership.

The LEGO Serious Play philosophy is fundamentally based on participatory leadership.

Whilst this is not a book about leadership, we would briefly like to advocate why LEGO Serious Play helps to address these all too common pitfalls.

LEGO Serious Play is a democratic and participative methodology that allows all meeting participants to first think actively alone, then tell a story of their

[3] An 'action strategy'. The motives, values or reasons that drive the way we act. For instance, if I were motivated by wanting to improve my performance, I'd seek and welcome feedback. If I were motivated by wanting to look good, I may control or limit the scope for negative feedback.
[4] Argyris & Schon, 1974, Theory in Practice

thoughts, before collectively reflecting upon the shared meanings of all points of view.

At the higher build levels LEGO Serious Play creates landscapes of all the 'agents' or factors that need to be taken into account.

The methodology allows groups to explore unintended consequences and recognise patterns to make it easier to decide upon courses of action and understand appropriate guiding principles.

All this from a product that was conceived as a toy, and has jumped a 'use category'.

To make an analogy it's a bit like the world wide web, a product initially devised to facilitate sharing and updating of information between researchers.

Who could have imagined in 1989 a geeky academic information exchange being used as it is today?

Just like the world wide web is no longer used only by academics, the bricks have also found their way to serious work.

A product designed for one purpose: play, has found another powerful and very serious purpose in work.

LEGO Serious Play is Serious Work

Some of us are judgemental. People might hear the phrase ' LEGO Serious Play' and think here comes the latest management fad. 'Uh-huh, oh-oh, OK'. And quite understandably that's what some participants body language says at the beginning of some workshops we run.

And whilst the occasional participant struggles with the process, the vast majority of sceptical participants revise their view after experiencing the power of LEGO Serious Play.

So one of the limits affecting this tool is an understandable judgemental perception of its name.

Yes the process uses LEGO® bricks.

Yes the process can be intensely and utterly absorbing for the PLAYer, and for sure it's focused on serious organisational concerns.

But this is not 'corporate TOY-Play', this really is Serious Work, hence the name of this book.

A facilitative mindset is the way of a participative leader.

The days are gone when one person controlled the flow of information. As Argyris and Schön suggested, this behaviour may occur unconsciously or involuntarily.

While being overly dominant in discussions leaders sadly, unintentionally and sometimes unbeknown to themselves silence others and keep information hidden.

Taking the lead, controlling the situation, having a confident assertive and clear point-of-view are often thought of as good qualities of an excellent leader.

However, these behaviours can also be accompanied with negative perceptions of being judgemental, pushy or opinionated.

The role that facilitative leaders take is different.

This mode of leadership usually assumes enquiry and exploration based behaviours.

Instead of telling what to do, they facilitate understanding about the subject-at-hand and allow people to find the best ways to adapt to the situations.

Instead of commanding, they share information and nourish learning between team members.

Instead of providing courses of action, they encourage and support learning of their colleagues.

Instead of pacing people along the predetermined path, they give them time to reflect and come up with their approach themselves.

Participatory, or facilitative leaders create conditions that allow all learning styles: activists, reflectors, theorists and pragmatists[5] to engage harmoniously with the subject-at-hand alone and as a group.

[5] Honey and Mumford, Learning Style Theory

This is the skill that can be learnt, most readily if the desire to learn is also underpinned by a genuinely held value:

The core value underpinning a facilitative mindset is to really want authentic, group wide participation.

To care about and be interested in what everyone really thinks, no matter the emotion of the person with a view or the diversity in a group.

And as it happens, LEGO Serious Play turns out to be rather brilliant at enabling participation.

LEGO Serious Play is one way that participatory leaders can facilitate teams to think and work together.

LEGO Serious Play, a participatory tool

LEGO Serious Play is based on five beliefs about leadership and organisations:

- Leaders don't have all the answers. Success requires all voices.

- People want to contribute, participate and take ownership.

- Allowing everyone to contribute creates a more sustainable business.

- Often, teams work sub-optimally, leaving team knowledge untapped.

- We live in a complex adaptive world, and need to see systemically.

Those five beliefs were established in the early years of the development of LEGO Serious Play, by the team at LEGO®, during the development of the LEGO Serious Play methodology.

They also happen to deeply resonate with our beliefs about participative leadership.

No. Let's not 'touch base'

There is no shortage of 'buzz phrases': fashionable but often meaningless 'turns of phrase' in business.

To try to ensure 'participatory leadership' does not become another meaningless buzz phrase let's look practically at what it means day-to-day in the actions of planning, leading or facilitating participatory meetings.

The International Association of Facilitators (IAF) has an excellent competency framework - standards that Certified Professional Facilitators have proven to work to in peer reviewed certification procedures.

As the IAF is a well kept secret, it's worth setting out briefly a summary of the six competencies, for as you'll see these are qualities that, by our definition, participatory leaders also have:

IAF six core competencies framework[6]

According to IAF, professional facilitators:

---

[6] This is an abbreviated version. See the full list at https://www.iaf-world.org/site/professional/core-competencies

A. Create collaborative relationships

Develop working partnerships and design and customise applications to meet client (or team) needs.

When you facilitate - don't participate!

One tension inherent in the idea of participatory leadership is the facilitation of something you have a strongly held opinion or emotional investment in. It is hard to both facilitate a group process at the same time as advocating your own strongly held view.

Of course the obvious risk is to pretend to facilitate, but actually manipulate the process to ensure the group accepts YOUR IDEA.

The very definition of opinionated, "characterised by conceited assertiveness and dogmatism," suggests there is little point in trying to facilitate a participatory processes if one cared little for others views or perspectives.

In circumstances like this external facilitators, either external to the organisation, or just not in your team or department can be of great help.

They should ensure your strongly held opinion is heard along with others, so you can explore what each others ideas might mean before seeking consensus.

B. Plan appropriate group processes

Select clear methods and processes and prepare time and space to support group process.

C. Create and sustain a participatory environment

Demonstrate effective participatory and interpersonal communication skills.

Honour and recognise diversity, ensuring inclusiveness, manage group conflict and evoke group creativity.

D. Guide groups to appropriate and useful outcomes

Use clear methods and processes, help groups be self-aware about the task and achieve consensus and clear desired outcomes.

E. Build and maintain professional knowledge

Maintain a base of knowledge and know a range of facilitation methods.

F. Model positive professional attitude

Practice self-assessment and self-awareness and trust group potential and model neutrality.

These are also six competencies of participatory leaders.

And as we hope you'll see from this book, LEGO Serious Play, with a few additional ideas from the experiences of professional facilitators, can be a method that rather effortlessly embodies most of these competencies.

Used with clear objectives, LEGO Serious Play is a way to improve communication and collaboration allowing all to participate in the work.

It brings energy and focus to meetings and workshops.

LEGO Serious Play enables the great potential of the collective untapped mind to create shared, and sometimes unexpected, insight in service of realising desired outcomes, of which, more in part 2...

Meeting Excellence Model

Excellent meetings:

are **Participative**, the right people giving full intellectual, emotional and energetic engagement.

are **Purposeful**, they motivate people with a compelling over arching purpose, and have specific and clear objectives.

have a **Process** designed to achieve the meeting objectives, maximising energy and diversity.

use **Visibility**, aligning the attention in the meeting and creating clear actions and learning.

are **Healthy**, they build authentic respect for each other and deliver real learning individually and collectively. This in turn creates an energetic, vibrant culture.

If your meetings are not excellent, you might ask 'how could we use these values as design principles for our future meetings?'

Next, we focus on desired outcomes

In part 2 we talk outcomes. Because that's what working together in meetings is all about.

Before we get into the nitty gritty of LEGO Serious Play, in part 3, we'll briefly advocate the importance of objective setting to plan meetings that create the outcomes you want.

Meeting Excellence Model: Core Principles of Excellent Meetings

Just like there is an excellent way to bake a soufflé, hit a golf ball or land an aeroplane, there is an excellent way to run a meeting.

The Meeting Excellence Model is based on theoretical and practical research. These principles apply to almost all kinds of meetings.

Participative
beliefs, underpinned by the participatory worldview
yield intellectual, emotional and energetic engagement.
Participation is the core principle.

Healthy
meetings create:
- authentic human respect
- deep, multi level learning
- an energetic, vibrant culture

Principles of **Meeting Excellence**

Purposeful
meetings have:
- a compelling overarching intention
- clear, specific meeting objectives
- focus, to achieve common objectives

Visibility
creates:
- aligned energy
- collective wisdom
- clear action and clear learning

Process
designed to:
- achieve objectives and get results
- maximise energy & participation
- harness diversity

These five principles, devised by author Sean Blair and inspired by facilitation industry best practice, have proven robust in more than ten years' worth of facilitation. You can think of these as the core values a facilitator, or participative leader has when working with groups of people.

Part 2

Outcomes not meetings

Outcomes not meetings

The objective of this chapter is to outline how to use clear objectives when planning meetings to create useful meeting outcomes.

Begin with the end in mind

Let's be honest. No one wants a meeting or workshop. What people really want is an outcome. This chapter makes the case that the planning stage of workshops is key to having effective meetings.

Objectives. Not agendas

The Oxford dictionary suggests the word 'agenda' has two meanings:

1. noun. 1. a list of items to be discussed at a formal meeting.

2. the underlying intentions or motives of a particular person or group

These two meanings are problematic for having effective meetings for two reasons:

1. "Discuss" a "list of items" is not a good way to have a productive meeting, and...

2. Unexpressed or *hidden underlying intentions or motives* do not make for a healthy meeting culture.

Verbs. Not verbiage

The verb in the dictionary definition of agenda is 'discuss'.

This is a horribly unhelpful verb, because if you invite a group to 'discuss' then that is exactly what they'll do.

This is the problem of agenda driven meetings...

Some will discuss what they think, others will share how they feel... Some might be seeking new information about the agenda item... One might be wanting to make a decision...

Another might be expressing support for the item, others might have questions or reservations, or be pursuing their own 'agenda' to 'put the boot in'.

And before you know it you have lots of people talking at cross purposes.

Nightmare

A better idea is to convert every agenda item to an objective with a thoughtfully selected verb.

This will help align group focus on all doing the same thing at the same time.

More on facilitating outcomes

You can also find additional facilitation tools, resources and LEGO® Serious Play® case studies (some reproduced in detail in this book thanks to the generosity of ProMeet's clients) at:

www.ProMeet.co.uk

Verbs determine process

Thoughtful selection of a verb also helps determine the process at any given part of the meeting.

'Decide verb?' - That needs a decision process.

'Create verb?' - That needs a creative process.

'Plan verb?' - That needs a planning process, and so on.

TRY THIS: With a forthcoming meeting, try and convert every agenda item into an objective. This preparation step will force you to think about what you want to have happen with each agenda item. See an example, page 53.

Clear objectives are the reason for meeting

Ideally, specific meeting objectives should connect obviously to the organisation's purpose and strategic objectives.

Well thought through objectives are more than half the work of planning an effective meeting. A clear objective implies the process design that follows.

Good objectives are stretching but achievable. When people are clear what is trying to be achieved, meetings work better.

The ProMeet method card on the next page describes how to write good objectives..

The ProMeet Objectives Logic

Create clear and productive meetings by establishing a clear objectives logic or hierarchy.

01: Objectives at the level of purpose
Organisations mission, vision or purpose

02: Objectives at the level of strategy
Organisations strategic objectives

03: Objectives at the level of the meeting
Clear, specific objectives the meeting is to achieve

Overcome meeting agony

Having asked thousands of people what is their version of 'meeting agony and ecstasy' we know that for many agony is when the purpose of a meeting is not clear.

Overcome this agony by using objectives, and banish agendas, in either sense of the word.

Accordingly, and like the example on page 53, for any kind of meeting or workshop (regardless of the methodology - LEGO® or no LEGO®) it is usually a wise idea to develop a clear objectives logic.

ProMeet Objective Setting Method Card

Download this Method Card @ www.serious.global/downloads

Use this Method Card as you plan your meetings. Convert every agenda item into an objective.

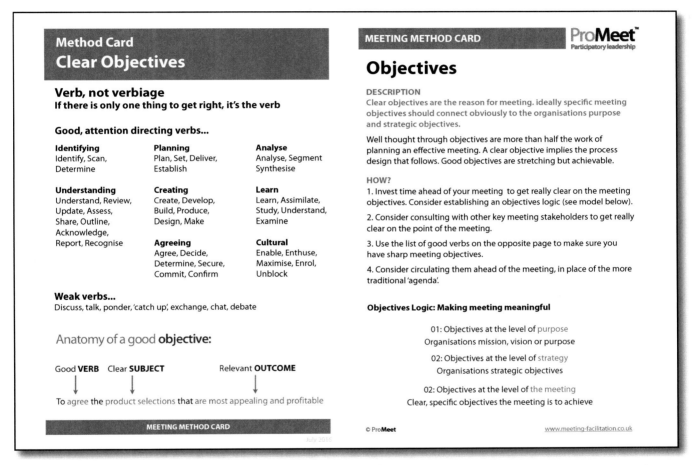

Method Card
Clear Objectives

Verb, not verbiage
If there is only one thing to get right, it's the verb

Good, attention directing verbs...

Identifying
Identify, Scan, Determine

Understanding
Understand, Review, Update, Assess, Share, Outline, Acknowledge, Report, Recognise

Planning
Plan, Set, Deliver, Establish

Creating
Create, Develop, Build, Produce, Design, Make

Agreeing
Agree, Decide, Determine, Secure, Commit, Confirm

Analyse
Analyse, Segment Synthesise

Learn
Learn, Assimilate, Study, Understand, Examine

Cultural
Enable, Enthuse, Maximise, Enrol, Unblock

Weak verbs...
Discuss, talk, ponder, 'catch up', exchange, chat, debate

Anatomy of a good **objective:**

Good **VERB**   Clear **SUBJECT**   Relevant **OUTCOME**

To agree the product selections that are most appealing and profitable

MEETING METHOD CARD

July 2016

MEETING METHOD CARD   ProMeet™
Participatory leadership

Objectives

DESCRIPTION
Clear objectives are the reason for meeting. ideally specific meeting objectives should connect obviously to the organisations purpose and strategic objectives.

Well thought through objectives are more than half the work of planning an effective meeting. A clear objective implies the process design that follows. Good objectives are stretching but achievable.

HOW?
1. Invest time ahead of your meeting to get really clear on the meeting objectives. Consider establishing an objectives logic (see model below).

2. Consider consulting with other key meeting stakeholders to get really clear on the point of the meeting.

3. Use the list of good verbs on the opposite page to make sure you have sharp meeting objectives.

4. Consider circulating them ahead of the meeting, in place of the more traditional 'agenda'.

Objectives Logic: Making meeting meaningful

01: Objectives at the level of purpose
Organisations mission, vision or purpose

02: Objectives at the level of strategy
Organisations strategic objectives

02: Objectives at the level of the meeting
Clear, specific objectives the meeting is to achieve

© ProMeet   www.meeting-facilitation.co.uk

A note on downloads: Many of the ideas in the book are supported with a set of document templates and PDF's that you can download, use and adapt for your own needs. They are freely available at www.serious. global/downloads You'll need to register an account first, then download all the assets referred to in this book.

Begin by getting clear on the overarching objectives; those at the level of purpose/vision or strategy, then establish the specific objectives of each session and 'agenda' item.

A common objectives framework uses the SMART acronym. Making every objective fulfil criteria of being Specific, Measurable, Achievable, Realistic and Time-bound.

Unfortunately this can make them also sound complicated. Our approach to objective setting is simpler and in line with everyday speak.

Allow preparation time

The example objectives on page 53 are from a real two day workshop for 30 people who flew in from different countries, and who did not spend much time working physically in the same room.

A costly and important meeting, it took some time and care to prepare the objectives and the workshop plan (or facilitation notes as we call them. You can see five examples in part 5).

A smaller meeting with less people demands less preparation time, but we'd still advocate using the objectives logic to ensure that participants are clear how what happens in the meeting connects to, and supports, a shared set of common organisational goals.

Smaller meetings with just a few participants with an hour or less is still worth preparing a set of objectives for.

Live Event Kick Off Workshop

O1: Overarching Objectives

1. To energise & inspire the delivery team to begin the new cycle feeling excited & motivated.
2. To develop ideas to make excellence - better.

These two overarching objectives will be met through delivering six sessions.

O2: Session Objectives

Session 1: To understand and enlarge the wellspring of inspiration the team can draw from.
Session 2: To strengthen the Live Event team.
Session 3: To develop shared understanding of our collective aspiration/vision for Live Event.
Session 4: To explore and generate ideas to improve participant experience.
Session 5: To attend to project hot topics and plan actions to address needs and concerns.
Session 6: To plan actions and share learning from our workshop.

O3: Meeting Objectives - Session 1: Inspiration
To identify, share and celebrate what we are proud of.
To understand and map the wellspring of inspiration of extraordinary face to face events, and life changing technologies.
To mine inspirational moments from other successful events (e.g. Glastonbury, Formula 1, Olympic finals, Burning Man etc.).

O3: Meeting Objectives - Session 2: Team Life
To appreciate and acknowledge the strengths our team has.
To share what is needed to be even more effective team members.
To understand what helps and hinders us from being a high performing and inspired team.

O3: Meeting Objectives - Session 3: Live Event Futures
To explore the aspirational identity of Live Event Futures, and create a shared mental model/vision of what we want to become.
To identify the 'agents' or factors that impact or are impacted upon by Live Event Futures, and explore risks and opportunities.
To create new pre event and post event service/value opportunities.

Etc ...

53

Plan for outcomes

When planning important meetings, a good preparation task is to ask key stakeholders these five questions. It can be done efficiently by giving participants a set of pre-printed A6 gridcards, a marker pen and three minutes.

Alternatively use A6 Post-It Notes (105mm x 148mm) or 4x6 inches (102mm x 152mm). It is also possible to cut A4 paper into 4 quadrants.

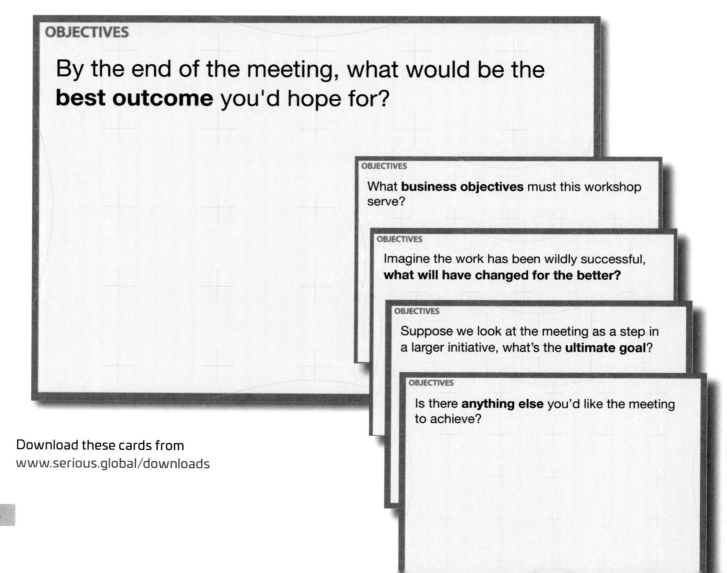

OBJECTIVES

By the end of the meeting, what would be the **best outcome** you'd hope for?

OBJECTIVES

What **business objectives** must this workshop serve?

OBJECTIVES

Imagine the work has been wildly successful, **what will have changed for the better?**

OBJECTIVES

Suppose we look at the meeting as a step in a larger initiative, what's the **ultimate goal**?

OBJECTIVES

Is there **anything else** you'd like the meeting to achieve?

Download these cards from
www.serious.global/downloads

Five great questions to ask when you're planning a meeting:

1. By the end of the meeting, what is the best outcome you'd hope for?

2. What are the Business Objectives this meeting must serve?

3. Imagine the meeting has been wildly successful, what will have changed for the better?

4. Suppose we look at the meeting as a step in a larger initiative, what's the ultimate goal?

5. Is there anything else you'd like the meeting to achieve?

What each of these questions is seeking to clarify or establish:

1. Above all, what key outcome should this meeting or workshop create?

2. Context. Establish the business or strategic objectives the meeting must serve.

3. Understand what change objectives this meeting needs to serve.

4. Understand what the purpose the meeting or workshop is in service of.

5. Understand if there are any other opportunities for the meeting to provide value.

See how these ideas were used in preparation for a half-day workshop with Manifesto Digital in the case study shown in part 5.5 on page 186 >>>

Example of how the planning questions were used to prepare the Manifesto team workshop...

At our meeting you suggested:

OBJECTIVES Imagine the workshops have been wildly successful. **What has changed for the better?**	PROCESS Imagine the workshops have been wildly successful. What has changed for the better? - Team engaged and 'own' the manifesto - Staff more engaged in the company, through taking more responsibility/ownership	PROCESS Imagine the workshops have been wildly successful. What has changed for the better? The team feel the company has a set a values and a Manifesto they created and believe in.
OBJECTIVES At the end of this work... **What is the best outcome you'd hope for?**	PROCESS At the end of this work... What is the best outcome you'd hope for? - Team more able to articulate our values to clients	PROCESS At the end of this work... What is the best outcome you'd hope for? People consider the values + Manifesto a core part of what it is to work at Manifesto and we all try to work towards them
OBJECTIVES Suppose we look at the workshops as steps in a larger initiative. **What's the ultimate goal?**	PROCESS Suppose we look at the workshops as steps in a larger initiative. What's the ultimate goal? More successful business with experienced team members	PROCESS Suppose we look at the workshops as steps in a larger initiative. What's the ultimate goal? An ongoing connection for new and existing employees with why we do what we do +/how

... And how the answers to the questions were translated into a set of workshop objectives.

Manifesto workshop

Overarching Objectives

To build a stronger team with shared values and agreed behaviours: "A new manifesto for Manifesto Digital".

Workshop Objectives

To share workshop objectives

To assess current level of team development

To build basic LEGO® Serious Play Skills

To share the 2017 Manifesto Vision with the team

To agree a lexicon for the workshop

To identify the core values of Manifesto

To identify the core positive behaviours Manifesto needs

To identify the core negative behaviours Manifesto does not need

To identify the Manifesto Simple Guiding Principles

To clarify what will happen next with this work.

To record the models in photos (Sean - over lunch).

Introducing facilitation notes

Facilitation notes are both a planning tool and a facilitator's roadmap.

Once the meeting objectives are clear, plan the step-by-step process and prepare your notes.

SERIOUS WORK

Overarching Objective To build a stronger team with shared values and agreed behaviours: 'A new manifesto for Manifesto.'			
Time	Session	Objective	Process/Notes
8:00	Set Up	**To get the room ready to support the needs of the participants and the workshop.**	Sean to set the room up to support the needs of the workshop. Set up to include • Screen/Computer/Speakers • 4 tables of 5/6 people • Tables for bricks • Tables for completed models
9:30	Arrival		9:00 for 9:30 start
10:00	Welcome & Objectives	**To share the workshop objectives.**	Jim to welcome Set the scene - run through objectives.
10:05	LEGO® Serious Play® Skills Building	**To build basic LEGO® Serious Play® Skills.**	**1. Technical - Build a model of a Tower** > Reflection: Use your model to tell your story Music – Snap out of it **2. Metaphors: Explain this! - use slides** > Reflection: You can make a brick mean anything Technical 'fancy' builds are not needed. Listen with your eyes! **3. Story telling: Build a model of your dream holiday** > Reflection: Trust and think with your hands, Tell the story of the model, not the one in your head. Music – Love Vibration

Plan successful meeting with facilitation notes

Overarching Objective: The objective the entire workshop is in service of. Getting this clear before defining the session objectives and process is key (see Part 2)..

In some cultures, time is a flexible concept. Add time at the beginning if you are in a country or culture where things tend to start late.

Session name: In organisations that need 'agendas,' when circulating before the meeting, use the first three columns (Time, Session and Objective). Don't circulate your notes

The objective for every session. A clear objective implies the required process.

Process column: A check list as you prepare. Notes when you facilitate.

Plan for success

After you have defined the objectives of your meeting, invest time planning for how those objectives will be met.

Download, edit or make your own version of our 'facilitation notes' template to design the process by which you'll lead or facilitate the group to achieve the desired outcomes.

There is much equipment and logistics involved in a LEGO® Serious Play® meeting. Think of facilitation notes as a planning tool or roadmap so you can have your attention on the people, not the process, during the meeting.

PROPER PLANNING PREVENTS POOR PERFORMANCE

Part 3

Beginning with LEGO® Serious Play®

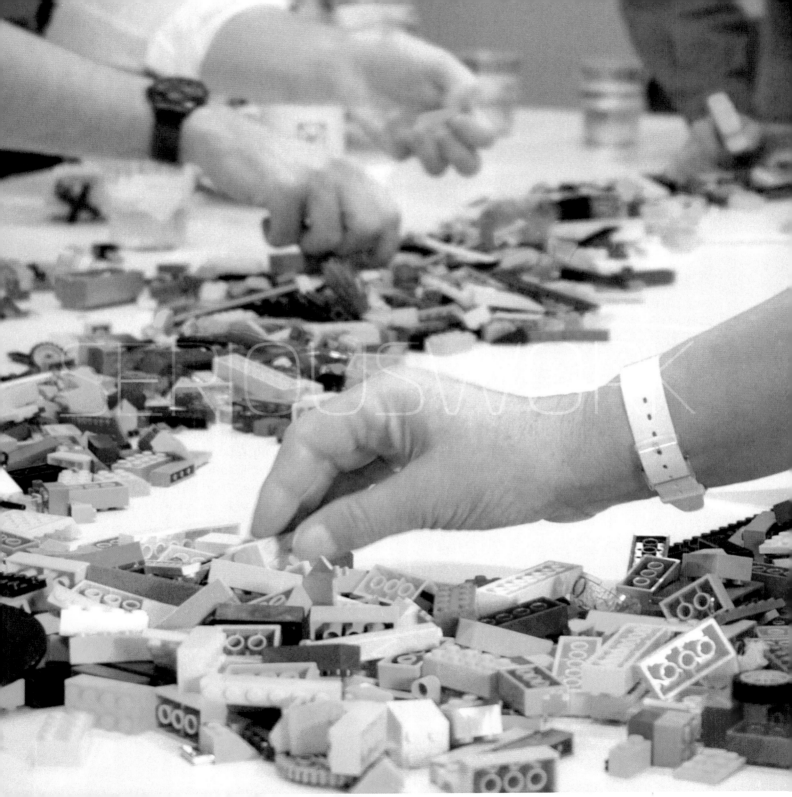

Beginning with LEGO® Serious Play®

The objectives of this chapter are:

To introduce you to the core ideas that underpin LEGO Serious Play

To provide information about which types of bricks are the best, where to get them and how to store them

A brief overview of LEGO Serious Play

In 2010 the LEGO Group created LEGO Serious Play Open Source and in doing so, kindly gifted the world a brilliant process. Thanks LEGO®!

The idea LEGO® had was to make the basic principles and philosophy freely available and support people wanting to use the process.

LEGO® produced an excellent Open Source guide that gives an overview of the process and how to use it. The creative common licence kindly allows everyone to share and adapt the ideas and processes, provided credit is given, a link to the licence is shared and changes are indicated.

For transparency, some sections of the guide appear below, with edits, to take into account our experiences.

What LEGO Serious Play is, and what LEGO Serious Play is not

According to the Open Source Guide:

The LEGO Serious Play methodology offers a sophisticated means for a group to share ideas, assumptions and understandings; to engage in rich dialogue to work out meaningful solutions to real problems.

A LEGO Serious Play workshop typically takes a day or, at its shortest, a workshop takes three or four hours. Unsurprisingly, as time is tight in business, and everywhere else, efforts have been made to reduce the length of time that LEGO Serious Play takes.

If a facilitator was to leave out the skills-building exercises and leap straight into a complex task and encourage participants to race through it, this would simply not be effective.

People using LEGO Serious Play methods have to recognise that the strengths of the process lie in its cycles of building, reflection, and collaborative learning. It is a facilitated process, used for particular purposes. Therefore, LEGO Serious Play is not a fun ice-breaker exercise to start off a meeting.

LEGO Serious Play is not a tool for building organisational diagrams or for planning physical environments (such as buildings or work spaces). Whilst you can use LEGO® bricks for these purposes, it is not LEGO Serious Play.

LEGO® Serious Play® Open Source Guide

The excellent LEGO® Serious Play® Open Source made available by the LEGO® Group under a Creative Commons licence 'Attribution Share Alike'.

For licence details: http://creativecommons.org/licenses/by-sa/3.0/

View a copy of the Open Source guide here: www.serious.global/downloads

The Core of LEGO Serious Play

LEGO Serious Play is a method that enables constructive reflection and dialogue.

During a structured process, participants use LEGO® bricks to create models that express their thoughts, reflections and ideas.

The 2010 Open Source Guide expressed a hope that the growing community of LEGO Serious Play facilitators would develop new applications for LEGO Serious Play.

The community has realised this aspiration. There are a hundred case studies of LEGO Serious Play on the www.seriousplaypro.com website, demonstrating it in use in a very wide range of applications, from anti-bullying and bible study, to business model canvas, service design and change management.

Process Steps

At the heart of LEGO Serious Play is a simple but powerful process that facilitators use. Slightly confusingly, the Open Source Guide offers both a three step and four step process that underpins the LEGO Serious Play method.

These processes are best summarised as:

1. Set the Challenge > 2. Build > 3. Share

1. Context > 2. Build > 3. Reflect > 4. Integrate

Rasmussen & Kristiansen (2014) suggest a 4-step "Core LEGO Serious Play process" 1. Posing the question > 2. Construction > 3. Sharing > 4. Reflection

Our experience led us to conclude that LEGO Serious Play meetings and workshops are most effective when following a six step process. Alternatively, you might think of it as a two + four step process.

Two vital steps take place in the preparation phase, and then there is a four step process during a workshop with participants, which is often repeated many times. A brief description of what happens in each step:

Phase 1: Establish objectives

Considering the purpose of the workshop in advance and developing a clear set of meeting or workshop objectives, as outlined in Part 2 of this book, is a prerequisite for any successful meeting or workshop.

Phase 2: Develop questions

Considering the purpose of the workshop in advance, the facilitator then formulates each building challenge in a way that will help release insight, open reflection and dialogue, and achieve the objectives.

The facilitator's choice and formulation of the building task or question is crucial for participants' experience of the process.

Facilitators LEGO® Serious Play® Process

Preparation Stage   Workshop stage

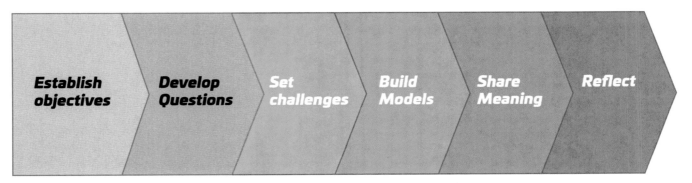

Establish objectives	Develop Questions	Set challenges	Build Models	Share Meaning	Reflect
Workshop process design should always be in service of a clear and relevant set of objectives.	Developing the right build questions is key. Even subtle changes in nuance can have a big impact.	The facilitator sets a build question or challenge.	Participants build LEGO® models representing their reflections on the building challenge.	Participants share the story of their own models, collectively the group explore the model and its meaning.	Groups reflect on what they have created and seek deeper layers of insight.

We suggest that a good core question fulfils four criteria:

- It has to be familiar and understandable for ALL participants;

- It needs to be important and engaging for ALL participants;

- It requires a combination of systematic and creative thinking;

- It ideally fosters different points of view among participants.

As we hope the brief story opposite shows, developing effective build questions is important. Even subtle changes in nuance can make a big difference to what people understand and what they then build.

Phase 3: Set Challenges

During the workshop, the facilitator issues the building challenge to the participants, the building time is made clear, and the facilitator asks participants to build a model with their LEGO® bricks that expresses their thoughts on, or response to the building challenge.

After offering the challenge, the facilitator gives examples to explain what they want participants to explore in their building.

Phase 4: Building

In this phase, participants build their response to the challenge with LEGO bricks. While building their models, participants assign meaning and narrative

Learning from mistakes: A lesson from Sean

"I recall a workshop where one of the objectives was to help the group think creatively and outside of an inward looking culture.

We wanted participants to imagine new possibilities that might arise from partnering with a completely new kind of organisation.

I instructed participants to **"Build a model of a new stakeholder; an unusual and mutually beneficial alliance partner who has an interest in providing an opportunity to engage with our clients."**

Looking back, this is not a great build question. It is complicated and unclear.

After the allotted build time was over, I invited participants to share the stories of what they had built. One participant began by saying she had found it hard and had got rather caught up with the word 'unusual'.

What I had meant to ask people to think of was new stakeholders, not unusual stakeholders. My use of the word unusual had really thrown at least this one participant and perhaps others.

Getting the build questions right is very important

Learning from Marko's mistakes. Not establishing clear build questions proves confusing.

Before being trained to facilitate LEGO® Serious Play®, my very first attempt was a Values Workshop. The client suggested that I introduce the theory about values before the workshop began.

To address this request, I gave a 1-hour extensively prepared lecture on the theory on what makes good values, including numerous case studies of the values agreed at similar firms.

After a long one-way lecture I finally asked the team: **"Now build good values with LEGO® bricks!"**

The session that followed was disorganized. Some tried to replicate what they had heard in the lecture. Others decided to build ideal values based on their personal experience. Yet another group thought that it would be best if they built the values of their organization. Yes, lots of time and energy got wasted in this confusion

Based on this experience I learned two lessons. First, beginning a LEGO® Serious Play® Workshop with too much theory constrains thinking.

Second, abstract "Build something" questions that don't support clear objectives create confusion.

Practise a build question

In Marko's situation, assuming he hadn't bored the bananas out of people for an hour before hand, what would have been a better build question to ask?

Jot below, or in a note book, better values build questions. Marko's answers below.

For instance: "Build the best behaviours that you have witnessed in your team."

or

"Imagine that the best values in your ideal team would be represented with a metaphor of an animal. Build this metaphor and explain it to others."

Both of those building tasks would have been more creative and fun, but at the same time more focused and objective oriented.

to their models by means of metaphors, figures of speech, and through story telling.

During building, individual participants reflect and gain a clearer and more detailed insight into their own reflections and thoughts. The building process both inspires and supports the reflective process, and participants are given a chance to think with their hands.

When participants use their hands to build three-dimensional models of their ideas, it gives them easier access to the knowledge and experience that is stored in their minds and catalyses new trains of thought.

Phase 5: Sharing

Next, participants share their stories with each other and assign mutual meanings to them.

It's vital that each participant shares the story about their model. One at a time, each participant shares the significance and story that they have assigned to their own model. The sharing might be a reflective process as when people share their models, they explore their own expressions more closely.

Those listening also have an opportunity to be curious and explore in more detail what the narrator expresses through the model.

The facilitator might ask questions during sharing with the purpose of getting participants to reflect and share more about their thoughts and ideas with each other.

Everybody shares what is on their minds and everybody is listened to. This is a very important purpose of LEGO Serious Play - to give everybody a chance to hear each others' points of view. When this happens, participatory leadership is alive and well.

Finally, sharing helps everyone feel ownership for the ideas expressed and take responsibility for the ideas generated. It is more likely that actions will follow.

Phase 6: Reflecting

After everyone has shared the story of their model and their individual insights, the facilitator asks the group to collectively reflect, for example on what patterns have been seen, what differences exist or what is the meta-story in the room now?

Participants' understanding of the process

During workshops, participants are not concerned with the preparation phase. It can be useful to explain the process to participants, typically during the skills build, in which case show participants the simpler four step process model opposite on an A3 board or slide.

LEGO® Serious Play® Participant Process

Download this A3 Board www.serious.global/downloads

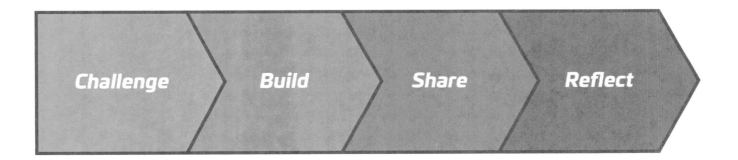

LEGO® Serious Play® Etiquette

Download this A3 Board www.serious.global/downloads

A facilitator sets the question/challenge, determines time lines & guides the process.

Your LEGO® model is your answer to the question/challenge.

There are no wrong answers.

Think with your hands. Trust your hands.

Tell the story of the model.

Listen with your eyes, as well as your ears.

Everyone builds, everyone tells..

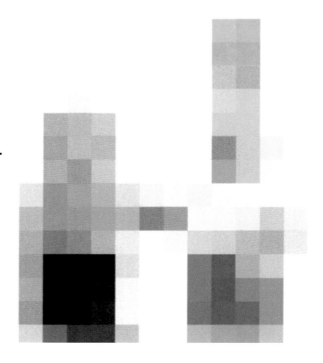

Participant Etiquette

Another useful idea in the LEGO® Open Source Guide that we have developed is participant etiquette.

Facilitators will find it helpful to make participants aware of the code of behaviour early on. In part 4 we suggest that facilitators inform participants about etiquette during the skills build.

With small groups it's more intimate to print the boards on to A3 card and use those as a visual aid. With large groups use a projected slide.

The facilitator poses the building challenges, sets the building time and guides the process.

The LEGO® model IS your answer to the building challenge, and...

There are no wrong answers. There is no right or wrong way to build. What the model looks like is not the most important thing. Invite participants not to judge their own models or more importantly, each others models.

Think with your hands: Tell participants 'If you get stuck after a challenge is set, trust your hands and just start building.' Encourage participants to let their hands do the thinking.

What counts is the meaning in the model and only the person who built the model knows what it means.

Tell the story of the model. It's vital that participants learn to communicate, share, and describe through the model, using the model. If the participant says that a model represents something specific, then that is what it is!

Sometimes participants build a model, then during the share they ignore it or pay scant attention to it and tell a story from inside their mind. With nothing but words to hold on to, it's amazing how quickly group attention drifts.

The challenge for the facilitator is to help those who do this to come back to the model and tell the model's story.

Listen with your eyes. Encourage participants to look at the model that is being shared and use their visual senses to grasp and understand even more of what the other participants are describing.

Everyone builds, everyone shares.
During the discussion that follows participants are free to ask questions about each others' models and stories.

Discourage people from expressing opinions about or interpreting each others' models or stories. Allow participants to ask questions about the model and the story - not about the person. The focus must be on the model and the story around the model rather than on the person describing the model.

LEGO® Serious Play® – Build Levels

There are three levels of building in LEGO Serious Play.

Level 1: Individual models is the foundation level.
Shared models and system models are built from
individual models.

**This book primarily focuses on the facilitation of
level one.**

LEGO® Serious Play® – Build Levels

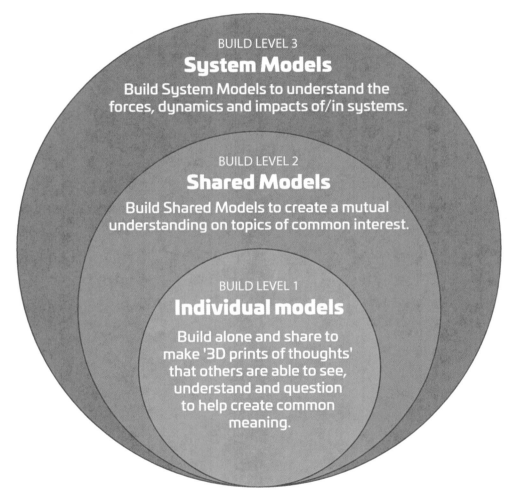

BUILD LEVEL 3
System Models
Build System Models to understand the forces, dynamics and impacts of/in systems.

BUILD LEVEL 2
Shared Models
Build Shared Models to create a mutual understanding on topics of common interest.

BUILD LEVEL 1
Individual models
Build alone and share to make '3D prints of thoughts' that others are able to see, understand and question to help create common meaning.

L3: Interact with dynamic systems. Understand how factors influence each other. Explore risks, opportunities and unintended consequences of different scenarios and strategies on shared visions.

L2: Explore how others see the same ideas differently. Then create shared understanding and common meaning

L1: Learn enhanced communication. Use auditory, visual and kinaesthetic modes to express your thoughts and feelings and understand the thoughts and feelings of others

Build Level 3 is not 'better' than Build Level 1. Level 1 is the foundation level and has huge power both alone and when combined with Build Levels 2 and 3..

LEGO® Serious Play® – Typical Applications & Build Levels

Download this A3 Board www.serious.global/downloads

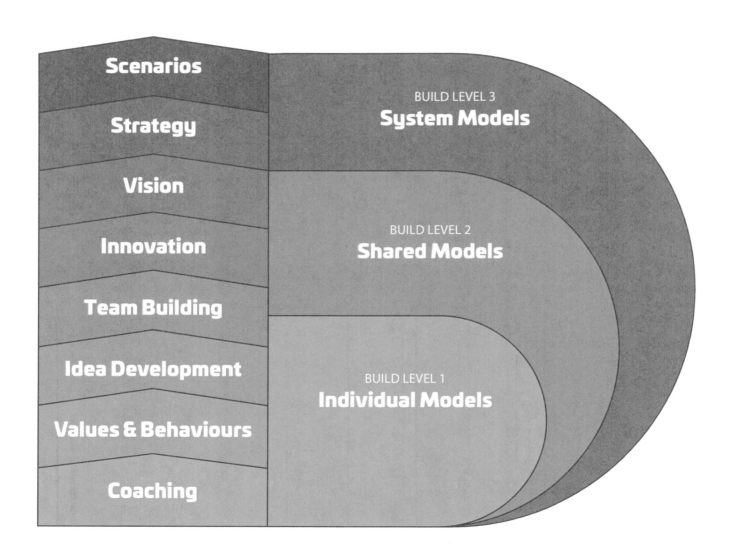

Scenarios

Strategy

Vision

Innovation

Team Building

Idea Development

Values & Behaviours

Coaching

BUILD LEVEL 3
System Models

BUILD LEVEL 2
Shared Models

BUILD LEVEL 1
Individual Models

Applications

LEGO Serious Play is just a tool. We think of it a bit like any other meeting tool, such as a flipchart and marker. Seen in this way the applications for LEGO Serious Play are as wide (wider actually!) as the humble pen and paper.

In organisational life there are common applications, some of which we cover in this book.

LEGO Serious Play Build Level 1 can be used in any meeting where you want everyone's input, where diverse thinking is welcome and where it is good to reflect before talking.

Level 1 (individual model building) is THE foundation build level. Even complex system models like the one shown below start from being built as Level One models.

A team using LEGO® Serious Play® to explore scenarios at Build Level 3 - System Models.

77

The Bricks

The aim of this section is to provide information about which type of bricks are best, where to get them and how to store them.

The bricks can be purchased at the LEGO® Shop:
http://shop.lego.com

LEGO® sell four LEGO Serious Play kits at its online store. These are special collections of bricks thoughtfully and carefully designed to help participants use metaphors and build simple models that can express complex ideas.

The brick selections in these kits are excellent. The kits contain bricks that you might not commonly find in children's LEGO® boxes, such as: money, ladders, meteors, plain Minifigures®, jet engines, flowers, pillars, plants, rotors and string. Whilst these bricks are not rare they enable a vast range of uses in LEGO Serious Play.

Should you rummage in your children's LEGO® boxes to try to assemble a kit, you might find character Minifigures® such as Batman, Bart Simpson, a cheerleader, or an evil henchman. It is hard for participants to use these bricks as they are already loaded with meaning.

Countries LEGO® ship to

The online LEGO® Shop http://shop.lego.com delivers to the following countries:

Australia	Germany	Poland
Austria	Hungary	Portugal
Belgium	Ireland	Spain
Canada	Italy	Sweden
Czech Rep.	South Korea	Switzerland
Denmark	Luxembourg	United
Finland	Netherlands	Kingdom
France	New Zealand	United States

If you don't live in a country that LEGO® ship to, there are some alternatives:

Bricklink

Bricklink is the world's largest online marketplace to buy and sell LEGO® parts. It stocks Minifigures® and sets, both new and used. LEGO Serious Play kits are available at Bricklink www.bricklink.com.

Assemble your own kits

While LEGO Serious Play standard kits are good, they are certainly not the only source of bricks. If you can't get LEGO Serious Play kits in your country you can make your own.

If LEGO® is available in local toy shops you can assemble your own kits by combining different kinds of LEGO® sets. Classic®, City®, Friends® and LEGO® DUPLO® bricks are the best sets to use.

Marko's article on 'do-it-yourself' LEGO Serious Play kits might be helpful:
seriousplaypro.com/bricks/diy/

Whilst Minifigures® can be seen as gender neutral, we have added a range of LEGO® Friends® characters to our sets to provide a better balance of gender and diversity.

LEGO® Friends® sets also contain animal, flower and plant bricks that are a useful addition to LEGO Serious Play brick sets.

eBay is a good source of bricks

Another option is to buy bricks on eBay, which is less costly than buying new bricks. Try the search term 'Bulk LEGO Bricks.' Typically 1kg of bricks cost £25.

Avoid buying second hand 'themed sets' unless you want a santa, a Wookie or R2D2 to become a central part of the stories your workshop participants share (trust us, you don't want that.)

We have bought additional base plates and Minifigures® from eBay to pad out the Landscape and Identity kits. These second hand bricks have worked out well.

What story does this simple model using LEGO Serious Play Starter kit bricks say to you?

Brief description of 4 kits

Windows Exploration Bag – Reference: 2000409

Starter Kit – Reference: 2000414

Photo © LEGO Group

Photo © LEGO Group

Contains: 48 bricks

See the inventory online at:

https://seriousplaypro.com/bricks/web/

Good for: Skills building, coaching and short workshops of up to half a day

Includes: A small selection of standard bricks in multiple colours and shapes.

Small selection of special elements and a Minifigure®

Contains: 219 bricks

See the inventory online at:

https://seriousplaypro.com/bricks/starter-kit/

Good for: Your first workshops, coaching, shared model building and general use

Includes: Selection of standard LEGO® bricks combined with a few LEGO® DUPLO® bricks. Also contains special elements such as wheels, tyres, windows, trees, two Minifigures®, tubes, globes and small base plates, Includes an 'imaginopedia' booklet with simple model building instructions for LEGO® skills building.

The next two kits are for Build Levels 2 and 3, and are for use in applications beyond the scope of this book. We suggest that you don't buy these kits without training first!

Landscape & Identity Kit – Reference: 2000430   **Connections Kit** – Reference: 2000431

Photo © LEGO Group

Photo © LEGO Group

Contains: 2631 bricks   Contains: 2455 bricks

See the inventory online at: See the inventory online at:

https://seriousplaypro.com/bricks/identity-kit/

https://seriousplaypro.com/bricks/connections-kit/

Good for: Build Levels 2 & 3 Workshops

Good for: System models at Build Level 3.

Includes: Large special mix of LEGO® bricks combined with LEGO® DUPLO® bricks, including animals.

Includes: Extensive selection of connecting elements such as spiral tubes, ladders, fences, bridges and strings.

Extensive selection of special elements such as wheels, tyres, windows, trees, 90 Minifigures®, sticks, globes, spiral tubes, ladders and fences.

Extensive selection of connectors making it possible to build a large interconnected LEGO® model.

Large selection of base plates and three orange plastic sorting trays

Ten identical bags containing specially chosen bricks that can be used for focused building exercises, such as "Pencil case," "Letter dog," or other exercises

Bricks to begin

As a very first step we'd suggest buying one starter kit to try some of the exercises yourself.

Photo © LEGO Group

For your first small workshop you can do a lot with one starter kit per participant, which for 6-8 people is not too big of an investment.

Alternatively you could buy two starter kits and add one box of Classic LEGO® kits (which are good value for money: LEGO® Creative Building Set Item: 10702), or some second hand bulk LEGO® from eBay (or even raid the LEGO® from any children in or close to your family. Be sure to remove themed bricks first!)

If you buy online, set up a LEGO® VIP Club account first to collect LEGO® points/money.

Now we've set the scene and covered the basic ideas, we will tell you how to facilitate a LEGO Serious Play Skills Build in part 4.

Learning from experience: Sean's big brickbox

I ran a large 3 hour workshop for 150 people. I gave each participant a brand new Windows kit and eventually they worked in groups of 4 to build shared models.

At the end of the workshop the new bricks were really mixed up, so I put them all in a big box.

A bit like making a big cake, I later added 12 starter kits to make a very big box of mixed LEGO® Serious Play® bricks.

I now use these bricks for many half and one day workshops. The day before a workshop I use digital kitchen scales to weigh and bag bricks in thick plastic zip close bags.

For a Skills Build and simple exercises, a table of 4 people would require 600g. For Shared Model building, I might later give the table another bag of 800g of bricks.

If you store the bricks in pillowcases they seem to air and stay cleaner than storing in plastic boxes.

This keeps a really great 'go-to' mix of bricks that suit many applications. It means I can keep my Landscape and Identity and Connections kits separate for multi-day strategy workshops

Put your bricks to work!

If you have some bricks (or when you get some) try this.

With a Window Exploration Kit, Starter Kit, or any random bricks you may have to hand, take a few minutes and have some fun.

Build a model to show the kind of leader you like working with. A person who gets the best out of you.

Interpret this build as you wish.

This ideal leader might be you. This leader may be somebody else you know well. This could also be a hypothetical person that does not exist.

After you have built your model, summarise its meaning with a couple of keywords.

Take a photo of your model and the keywords and share it with us.

Send your photo via Twitter to @SeriousWrk.

We would be glad to learn from you.

What kind of leadership qualities do you consider important?

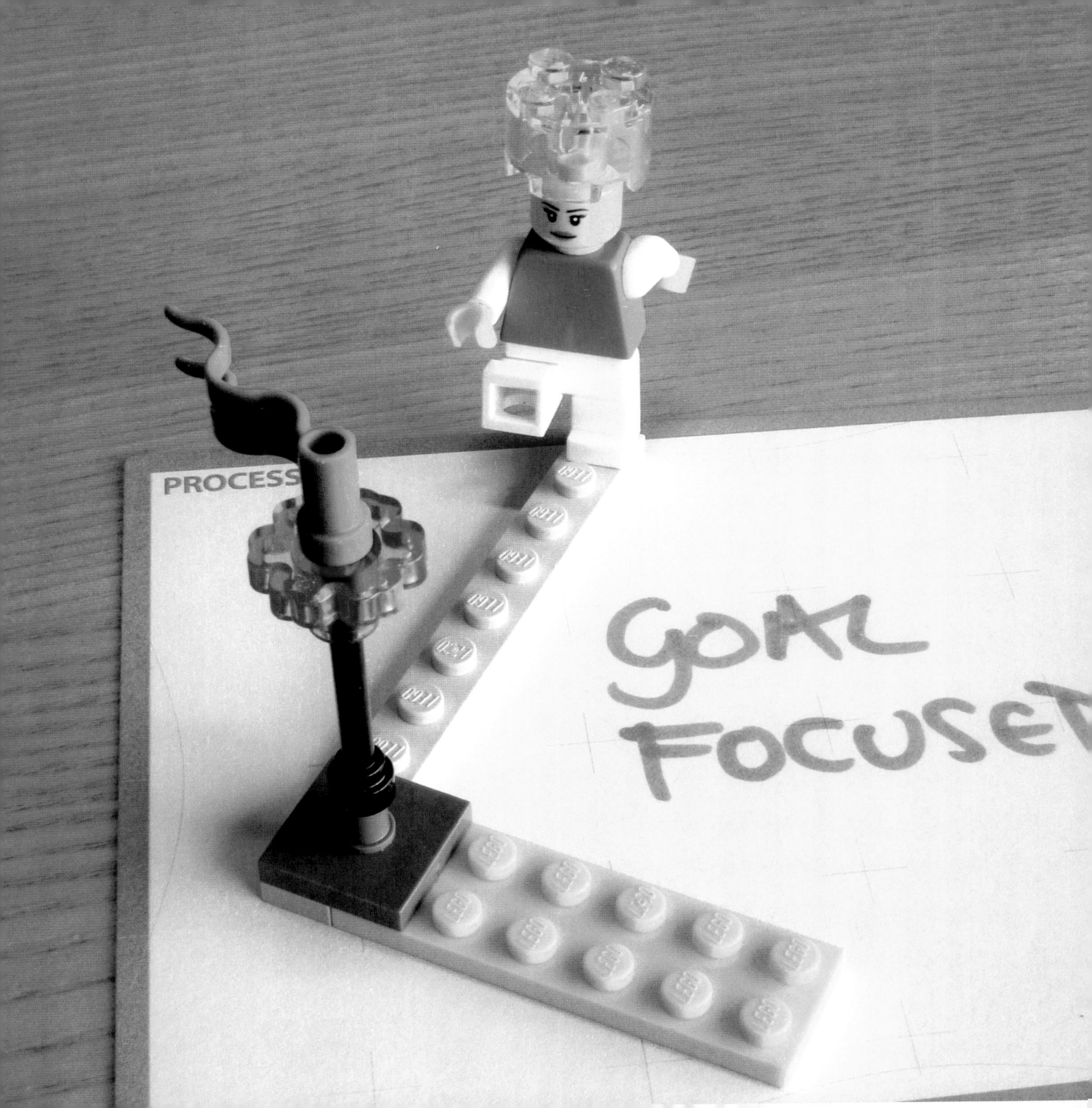
PROCESS
GOAL

Part 4

LEGO® Serious Play® skills build...

... & Four Fundamentals

The absolutely, fundamentally vital things that LEGO®
Serious Play® facilitators do.

LEGO® Serious Play® Skills Build

The objectives of this chapter are:

To enable you to facilitate a LEGO® Serious Play® Skills Build

To understand how the LEGO Serious Play Facilitation Fundamentals achieve enhanced communication

Why a Skills Build?

The LEGO Serious Play Skills Build is a foundation component of the LEGO Serious Play method. Don't even consider skipping it. Not ever.

The Skills Build gives participants technical, metaphor and story telling skills, whilst enabling them to use the bricks as adults engaged in LEGO Serious Play as opposed to children involved in play.

The Skills Build is also the time to normalise how participants should use the bricks with the enhanced communication that LEGO Serious Play makes possible.

Some people come to a LEGO® Serious Play® workshop feeling unsure or sceptical about being confronted with what looks like a kids toy set. This can make them think negatively and feel uncomfortable. Done well, the skills build will help even hardcore sceptics experience the power of LEGO Serious Play and dissolve the reticence that is visible if you have a room full of people leaning back on their chairs, arms crossed, looking bemused.

Learning from experience: Sean's story

I was facilitating a workshop to help develop a youth engagement strategy for a UK charity.

At the outset I saw crossed arms and one or two people looked uncomfortable.

After we completed the Skills Build I asked the group for reflections.

One participant, who had not initially looked at ease, with a smile and a twinkle in her eye, said, *"You know what? This isn't as naff as I thought it would be."* ('naff.' British slang, describing something that is stupid, lame or unpalatable).

I loved that she said that and thanked her for it. She said what others too had thought. Her experience of being really listened to in the Skills Build legitimised the process in her mind. She was now 100% onboard with the process.

SERIOUS WORK

Skills build 1: The Tower

Two components

The Skills Build has two components.

1. Giving participants technical, metaphor and story telling skills.

2. Normalising the enhanced communication that LEGO Serious Play makes possible.

In this chapter, we'll give you a typical workshop plan/set of facilitation notes that you can download and adapt for your own workshop.

How long is a Skills Build?

For small groups of about 8 people allow 40-60 minutes to deliver a Skills Build.

Some facilitators allocate up to 90 minutes for a Skills Build, but for short workshops that are three to four hours in duration it's hard to give about half the workshop time to the skills build when participants are rightly keen to explore their issues. Done well, a Skills Build can enable even large groups to successfully use LEGO Serious Play in 30-40 minutes.

In Part 3, Beginning with LEGO Serious Play, we outlined the LEGO Serious Play process steps (page 71) that included a 'shared meaning' stage. In this stage, participants tell the stories of their models. Clearly it will take a group of 10 people about twice as long to do this as a group of 5 people.

The Skills Build typically has three exercises, and so the majority of the time is used for participants to tell the stories around their models. What you ask participants to build and how tightly you control the 'share time' will determine much of the total duration is spent on a Skills Build.

Group size

In your early days of practising LEGO Serious Play aim for a smaller group size. The general rule is one facilitator to a maximum group of 12 participants.

There are advanced techniques to facilitate large groups but begin by learning to facilitate small groups of about six people.

What bricks should I use?

The ideal set of bricks for the Skills Build are the Windows Exploration kits (art.2000409). The small bags are not too expensive individually and they contain a super mix of 48 bricks. The only downside is you have to buy them in boxes of 100 bags.

An advantage of using these kits is that everyone has the same bricks. With care it is also easy to ask participants to put the bricks back afterwards into zip close bags for future use. If you don't want to buy a box of 100 bags, you have two options:

A Windows Exploration Kit

Perfect for the skills build, if you don't mind buying a box containing 100 bags.

Option 1. From a well mixed random selection of small to medium sized bricks, weigh out about 80-100g and make individual bags.

Option 2. Place a pile of small to medium sized bricks in the middle of table in reach of all. As a rough guide aim for 100g of LEGO® bricks per head.

Skills 1: Technical: Build a Tower

The first Skills Build seeks to give participants the technical skills of connecting bricks.

Be aware that older hands and eyes can find the smaller LEGO® bricks fiddly. Pay extra attention to the Technical Skills Build with older groups.

A perfect first Skills Build task is to ask people to build a model of a tower. We all have a mental model of what a tower might look like, and how people interpret the build also helps us learn something about how they think or perceive.

Skills 2: Metaphor: Explain this!

Learning to use bricks as metaphors liberates people to tell rich stories with simple builds.

We sometimes point out the way in which children use LEGO®, which is to try to build models that look like an idea in their minds. The polar bear example opposite illustrates the point.

A LEGO Serious Play participant does not need to build a model of a thing to be able to tell a story about the thing. They can use a brick as a metaphor.

We often use a simple game called 'explain this' (described in the facilitation notes that follow.)

The game forces participants to give their bricks a meaning and quickly helps free participants from feeling limited to using the bricks literally (though literal meaning is useful too!)

LEGO Serious Play goes beyond using LEGO® bricks to build models representing items or material objects in the real world.

LEGO Serious Play can be used to create models of your thoughts. Therefore, it helps to create solid 3D prints of your ideas using metaphors.

For instance, the polar bear could symbolise something "strong, forceful and Nordic."

It is up to the facilitator to help participants come up with a meaning for the bricks that they used and convert it into an appropriate metaphor.

Using Bricks as Metaphors

Helps participants tell rich stories with simple builds.

How artist Sean Kenney represented Polar bears in LEGO® (serious LEGO® skills!).

©Sean Kenny 2016

How a child might represent a LEGO® Polar bear.

How a Polar bear could look or be represented in a LEGO® Serious Play® Workshop.

Marko's thematic "Explain this!"

There are several ways to play "Explain this!" The facilitation notes on page 104 invite participants to build random models and explain that these mean something, e.g. "marriage, weather or genetic engineering."

I also use the "Explain this!" task in a thematic way to help people think about the concept they will be shortly working on. For example:

– for a team building workshop I ask them to use their random buildings to explain: "team, colleague or friendship"

– for a strategy workshop: "future, goal or achievement"

– for an identity workshop: "my alter ego, my deeper self, or when I was a child"

– for a product development workshop: "client's wish or a cool new product"

– for an innovation workshop: "R&D or a technology breakthrough"

It's great fun and effective. People realise that they are able to take their random building and explain something about the topic they know well. Thinking about the upcoming concepts of the workshop during a Skills Build will set a positive scene for the upcoming workshop.

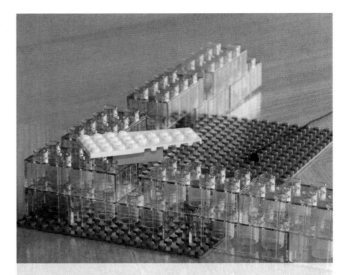

Bricks as Metaphors
1. Rising Sea Levels

Bricks as Metaphors
3. Bird Flu

Bricks as Metaphors
2. Climate Change

Bricks as Metaphors:
4. Increased Diversity

The examples opposite are from an environmentally and socially minded group. They had been asked to build 'agents' (factors that would impact or be impacted on by their vision) in a Build Level 3 system model.

These photos show differing levels of metaphor. In photo 1, the LEGO® DUPLO® bricks with a white base plate on top symbolised rising sea levels: a simple build of just a few bricks to represent a big concept. Photo 2 looks like a palm tree, but in this build it represented climate change. Photo 3 is more literal, representing bird flu. Photo 4 symbolised increasing diversity in society.

Skills 3: Story Telling

Story Telling helps create memories that stick. Even months and years later participants can remember what was said as workshop participants used their models to tell rich and entertaining stories.

Story Telling using the models is the root of the 'enhanced communication' that LEGO Serious Play enables. This skill requires the story teller to use the model and the listener to listen with eyes and ears. There are four fundamentals you must master.

Four Facilitation Fundamentals

The four facilitation fundamentals described next are vitally important conditions that you as a facilitator must help create. These are unique to LEGO Serious Play.

Fundamental 1: Enable the three modes of Enhanced Communication

People find communication is more effective with LEGO Serious Play because it facilitates auditory, visual and kinaesthetic communication.

These three modes allow a speaker to communicate more fully by 1) explaining the idea with words, 2) explaining what each brick in the model means and 3) moving and articulating the model, describing it from different perspectives.

In LEGO Serious Play Workshops you lose visual and kinaesthetic communication the moment a participant moves their attention away from the bricks and starts to present a thought-based story. Then the listeners visibly begin to zone out.

Your job as a LEGO Serious Play Facilitator is to help people quickly learn how to use the bricks as an enhanced form of communication and help them constantly focus their attention on bricks.

Fundamental 2: Help participants tell the story of the model

The most common pitfall of LEGO® Serious Play® is when participants don't tell the story of the model they have created.

The Skills Build is a vital stage to help participants understand the central importance of telling the story of the model and activating the three modes of communication.

From the very first warm up task, and during every round of sharing, bring participants attention to the core ideas.

'Tell the story of the model.' 'Touch and point.' 'Listen with your eyes.' 'Be curious about what each others models mean.'

Acknowledge participants who do these things well to develop these group habits. Watch for people who build models and don't use them to tell the story, help them focus!

Politely but firmly establish this practice during the Skills Build. It will help a lot later.

Fundamental 3: Establish listening with eyes as the norm

Listening is hard. In most meetings people do not listen well. LEGO Serious Play can be a huge help in overcoming this common problem.

Listening in LEGO Serious Play Workshops is also more effective than traditional 'speech only' communication as the listener can use their eyes as well as their ears to see and hear what's meant.

Suggest that when this is happening you'd expect to see every set of eyeballs in the room focused on the part of the model that is being explained.

Encourage speakers not to make eye contact with others but instead focus their own attention on the part of the model they are explaining.

As a facilitator, when you observe a whole group listening with their eyes, point out and reward the positive behaviour and ask what it was like for the speaker to be heard.

Fundamental 4: Encourage curiosity about the models

When speakers tell the story of their model and listeners listen with their eyes, you'll enable all participants to become curious about the meaning.

The models allow listeners to interrogate **deeper layers of meaning**. Remember the LEGO Serious Play Etiquette and encourage participants to be curious about the models.

Deeper layers of meaning can be unveiled by asking questions such as: 'Does the blue brick on the top mean anything?' 'What does the flower on top of the flag mean?'

Make it OK for there to be no meaning to these parts if there is none, but encourage speakers to express other meanings that their models might have. Don't allow listeners to give new and different meanings to the speakers model.

As a facilitator, your job is to help the group have a meaningful exchange. Be curious and encourage curiosity.

The Skills Build is THE time and place to embed the practices these facilitation fundamentals demand.

Summary: LEGO® Serious Play® Facilitation Fundamentals

You'll enable three modes of enhanced communication

You'll help participants tell the story of the model

You'll establish listening with eyes as the norm

You'll encourage curiosity about the models.

Sharing Models: Enhanced Communication.
The model at the centre of the stage.

Imagine you're presenting your model (not in this workshop), but on a stage ...

Put your model centre stage.

Download this A3 Board www.serious.global/downloads

Be like a director, narrator or puppet master and have the model **centre stage** as the total **focus** of the audience's attention.

Don't look at the audience or make eye contact with them, as this brings their attention away from the model and on to you, an invisible director.

Focus your eyes totally on your model.

Tell the story of the model: Use auditory, visual & kinaesthetic communication... like a puppet master, **speak, show and animate** your model. Bring it to life.

... if you do this well the audience will have **no choice** but to **listen with their eyes and be curious about your model**.

Practise

We strongly suggest that you practise this Skills Build two or three times in a safe, low risk environment before trying to facilitate any important meeting or workshop. Download the facilitation notes as a word document and edit them for your own needs ahead of the workshop.

It is good practice to try and do the builds you will ask participants to perform ahead of the workshop. You might learn something useful and further modify your plan ahead of the workshop with participants.

Perfect practise makes perfect

There is a subtlety to facilitating in a way that controls but doesn't feel controlling. To master these skills consider practise based peer learning by attending a training course. See Part 7 of this book to assess which types of training will give you the skills you need.

Facilitation notes

The facilitation notes and narrative in the pages that follow describe a typical LEGO Serious Play Skills Build. The timings have been optimised for a group of 6 people and the workshop should take up to an hour. You might get other ideas or see these ideas brought to life in the five facilitation notes in Part 5.

N.B.: The only time it is OK to skip Skills Build is if you are working with a group where ALL members have LEGO Serious Play skills.

Learn from experience: Sean's story

I had been working with an organisation to help them improve their leadership culture and meeting practices.

At the outset we began with a LEGO® Serious Play® workshop that created a vision for their leadership team of seven people. This of course had begun with a LEGO® Serious Play® Skills Build.

Some months later they were reviewing their business plan. Written on the front page of the draft plan were their 'organisational values.' The values were not those that I had seen in action and so I challenged the group, and they agreed that they were not accurate.

I had some LEGO® kits in my bag so I suggested a 2 minute individual build of the key value they felt they needed to deliver in the business plan.

After each person had built and told the story of their models (I summarised the key ideas on cards at the same time), I gave each of them three bricks to vote for the values they thought were the strongest. The whole intervention took less than 10 minutes and an agreed set of the right values had been established

Objective: To give participants LEGO® Serious Play® skills – allow 60 minutes			
Time	Session	Objective	Process/Notes
30 mins The timing here is based on 6 people	Set Up	**To get the room ready to deliver the workshop.**	Equipment: • Facilitation notes • LEGO® Bricks - comfortably accessible, either in bags, in a pile, in a horseshoe shape or in a circle • Timer or stopwatch (use a phone app) • 'Explain this' cards (www.serious.global/downloads) • A3 Explainer Boards (www.serious.global/downloads) • Optional music
1 min	Welcome	**To make participants feel comfortable and legitimise any scepticism.**	A 'from the heart' welcome that is right for the culture of the group Sometimes it is useful to explicitly 'make it OK' for participants to feel unsure or even sceptical about being confronted with LEGO® Ask people to trust the process and have an open mind about LEGO® Serious Play® for the next hour.
2 mins	Objectives	**To clarify the workshop objectives.**	Begin by establishing the workshop objectives and workshop plan or roadmap.

Facilitation notes *narrative*

A 'standard' set of facilitation notes for a skills build with a small group of about six people.

Allow time to set up the room. Make sure the tables are clear of anything apart from bricks, as this helps people to see the small models.

Music. Consider creating a playlist of tracks lasting 2-3 minutes that work well for some of the build tasks. We use a bluetooth speaker with an iPad.

Music seems to help participants concentrate on the build task and you can use short tracks as a countdown. You can, for example, say 'You've got until Elvis finishes singing to complete your model...'.

In almost all cases, the Skills Build is the first part of a workshop to explore a particular issue.

Good practice would be to ensure people arrive with an understanding that LEGO® Serious Play® will be a process tool used in the workshop.

This Skills Build used a mix of LEGO® Serious Play® Windows Kits and Starter Kits that were spread out in a horseshoe within arms reach for each of the 12.

Download this workshop plan & template:
www.serious.global/downloads

Objective			
To give participants LEGO® Serious Play® skills			
Time	Session	Objective	Process/Notes
c.12 mins (1 min frame 2 mins build + 2 mins boards 1 min share each)	Skills 1: Technical Tower Build Tower Share Tower Reflect	To give participants technical skills and confidence to use the bricks.	**1. Challenge: Frame the task.** *The first task is simple; to get used to connecting the bricks* *TASK: "You have 2 minutes to Build a Tower".* **Start timer and or play music** Music: Elvis v JXL, A Little Less Conversation **2. Build:** After 1 minute say to the participants: 'You have 60 seconds remaining'.. After 2 minutes ask if anyone needs more time and invite people to stop building **3. Share:** Tell participants: *'It's hard to listen to what others are saying if you are still building, so are you all ready to hear each other's stories?'* **> Facilitator Instructions:** 1. Encourage people to tell the story of the model; pick it up, point to and touch each part. 2. Encourage all to listen with eyes and ears **4. Reflect:** *'What reflections do you have?'* You might want to offer these additional reflections: Simple build. Every model is different. No wrong answers.

Facilitation notes *narrative*

The first task – to build people's technical skills.

The first task is intended to get participants comfortable with connecting the bricks, following the core process and learning how to use the models in 'enhanced communication.' Usually, some participants are familiar with LEGO® and others have not used LEGO® for a while, if ever.

Elvis is entirely optional.

Start the share step by showing participants the A3 'Core Process' and 'Etiquette' boards. These will help participants to understand the four steps of the core process and locate the current task within this and etiquette.

LEGO® Serious Play® Core Process   SERIOUS **WORK**

Challenge   Build

LEGO® Serious Play® Etiquette   SERIOUS **WORK**

A facilitator sets the question/challenge, time lines & guides the process.

Your model is your answer to the question/challenge.

There are no wrong answers.

Think with your hands. Trust your hands.

Tell the story of the model.

Listen with your eyes, as well as your ears.

Everyone builds, everyone tells.

Begin to embed the 'Facilitation Fundamentals' and encourage participants to use the Enhanced Communication techniques. Encourage the person telling the story of the model. Ask people who don't use their models what specific bricks mean.

If you use Windows Exploration Kits (see Part 3), ask people to only use the black base plate and green and orange bricks (photo page 89). Limited brick choice helps show that the same bricks produce very different results.

Objective **To give participants LEGO® Serious Play® skills**			
Time	Session	Objective	Process/Notes
c.10 mins (1 min frame 1 min build + 2 min explain 30 secs share each)	Skills 2: Metaphor Explain This!	To enable participants to use the bricks as metaphors.	**1. Challenge: Frame the task.** *The second Skills Build helps us learn how to use the bricks as metaphors. You can think of it as a game called Explain This!* *To begin let me set the challenge* **2. Build** *TASK: "You have 30 seconds to connect 5 bricks together in a random and meaningless way. Any bricks, any connections, just a random 5 brick model."* **Start timer** **When everyone has a 5 brick model explain how the bricks can be used as metaphors** Introduce 'Explain This!' **3. Share: One by one, give people a card and invite them to explain their models.** > **Facilitator:** Validate the stories people tell! **4. Reflect:** *'What reflections do you have?'* Offer additional reflection: You can make a brick mean anything

PROCESS

Please imagine the 5 brick model you have built is a representation of...

Space Travel

Explain this!

Facilitation notes *narrative*

The second task - to teach people how to use bricks as metaphors.

Invite people to recycle their towers before you begin this task.

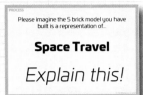

www.serious.global/downloads

Explain how children often use LEGO. They try to build models that look like ideas in their mind. Find a single white 4x2 brick and explain that you could use this brick to represent a Polar Bear (see page 89).

You don't need to build a model of a bear because you can use a white brick as a metaphor for a bear. Equally you could use the same brick to mean 'Good Health,' 'Cake' or 'Democracy'. This is using the brick as a metaphor.

Give each participant a card. The card has a word or two with an object, concept or idea written on it. The participant has to tell the other participants what the concept is, then explain the concept on the card using the model they have built. Depending upon what the model looks like and how agile their imaginations are, some participants will find 'Explain This!' easier, some will find it harder. That's OK.

If anyone gets totally stuck you can ask if there is someone in the group who is willing to try and explain the concept with the model either they have built or using the model of the person who's stuck. Alternatively, you can step in and explain the model.

It gets easier as you go on as people learn how to play the game. To finish, compliment the participants by reflecting that anybody could speak about anything in front of a group without any preparation.

Objective			
To give participants LEGO® Serious Play® skills			
Time	Session	Objective	Process/Notes
c.20 mins (1 min frame 3 min build + 2 min explain 1-2 mins share each	Skills 3: Story Telling	**To enable participants to use models to tell stories and embed the enhanced communication techniques**	**1. Challenge: Frame the task.** The final Skills Build helps us learn how to use our models to tell stories **2. Build** *TASK: "You have 3 minutes to build a model to tell a story about..."* **Start timer and/or play music** Music: Pharrell Williams - Happy. **Count down... 2 mins remaining... 1 min remaining... does anyone need more time?** **3. Share: Ask people to share the stories about their models** **> Facilitator Instructions:** Encourage people to be curious about each others' models **4. Reflect:** *"What reflections do you have?"* Trust and think with your hands; tell the story of the model > Be interested in each others' models
5 mins	Reflections	**To invite participants to share reflections from the Skills Build**	After the final Skills Build, ask people what reflections they have. What do they think about LEGO® Serious Play® now? What worked well or was hard?

Facilitation notes *narrative*

The final task - to teach people how to use models to tell stories and embed the Four Facilitation Fundamentals.

Set a build task that gets the group in the mood for what will follow.

Question/Task Design. You have choices in this task. You can ask participants to build a model to tell a story about, for example, a dream holiday, a nightmare boss, a hidden skill I have, what I'm most proud of achieving personally or professionally etc.

You might not choose the 'nightmare boss' task if the room has bosses in it, but if you want the group to work with critical insight you could, for instance, ask people to build a model of a nightmare neighbour.

If the last thing you want is to unleash a group's critical power, then you might focus on positive things, such as dream team members or things I am proud to have achieved etc.

This is another opportunity to try and embed the Facilitation Fundamentals and Enhanced Communication techniques. By this stage you will know which participants naturally model the appropriate behaviours according to LEGO® Serious Play® etiquette.

Consider asking someone who has this skill to begin. After they have told the story of their model bring the group's attention to what happened and say that's how it should be done.

If someone does not tell the story of their model/use the techniques you have introduced, watch the attention of the group drift. Without highlighting that the person was wrong, point out what happened.

Be curious about the models and encourage others to ask what different bricks or relationships between bricks might mean.

Part 5

Workshop applications and case studies

5.1 Goal setting workshop

5.2 Team build - FutureLearn

5.3 Ideas workshop - Telia Telco

5.4 Values & behaviours - Manifesto

5.5 Shared vision - IHG

Workshop applications

The objective of this chapter is to enable you to facilitate five common workshop applications.

Build Level 1: Individual Model Case Studies

The case studies that follow are focused on Build Level 1, but the Shared Vision case study in part 5.4 gives you a very brief overview of Build Level 2: Shared Models.

Our case studies start with a simple application and we then illustrate more complex applications

Case study structure

In each application we give you the background story, then offer you the workshop plan from these projects that we have facilitated using LEGO® Serious Play®. We have annotated the facilitation notes to describe how to prepare for, run and follow on from these workshops.

We offer you these case studies so you can see how these ideas were applied in practice and what outputs and outcomes were created. You can download these facilitation notes at www.serious. global/downloads and edit and adapt them for your own use.

Use... but plan for *your* needs

As a point of emphasis, we don't advocate that you should take these plans and run these workshops exactly as we did. We offer you these resources to help you prepare for and run your own workshops.

To deliver a successful workshop, firstly, and most importantly, use our ideas about the preparation phase to establish an objectives logic and translate your objectives into a workshop plan.

The vital preparation phase helps you develop a shared understanding with key workshop stakeholders or clients on the objectives and process to create the desired outcomes.

Once clear meeting or workshop objectives have been established, you're ready for Step Two.

Prepare your facilitation notes as your minute-by-minute guide to use during the workshop.

Now let's look at how LEGO Serious Play was used in five different workshops.

The case studies focus on Build Level 1 applications

Scenario

Strategy

Innovation

Vision

Team Building

Values & Behaviours

Idea Development

Coaching

BUILD LEVEL 3
System models
Build system models to understand the forces, dynamics and impacts of and in systems

BUILD LEVEL 2
Shared models
Build shared models to create mutual understanding on topics of common interest

BUILD LEVEL 1
Individual models
Build alone and share to make '3D prints of thoughts' that others are able to see, understand and question to help create common meaning

Part 5.1

A Goal Setting Workshop

Goal Setting Workshop

1 person, 1 hour

Background

In this starter case study we share a one-to-one goal setting workshop which is a great first session to try with a friend or workmate.

Your first LEGO® Serious Play® session needs an informal setting and a friendly counterpart. This way you feel relaxed and can be at your best in a low-risk environment. Ask a friend to be your "client," reserve one hour and you are good to go.

Compared to other LEGO Serious Play applications, one-to-one sessions pose modest requirements for space. You could do it in an office, a cafeteria or a hotel lobby. As long as you and your client both feel comfortable, any place will do. Just a small table where you can stack some bricks is enough.

If the space allows, place the chairs side-by-side or at an angle to allow you both to interact with the landscape of LEGO® models that will be built during the workshop.

Use a LEGO Serious Play Starter Kit and have a notebook and pen to record key ideas. Use clear handwriting, so when the session is about to end, you can review the summary of the notes together with the client.

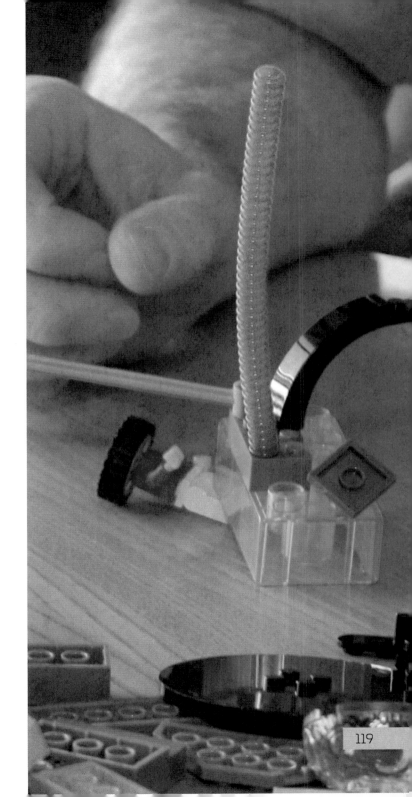

Overarching Objective Set goals and create an action plan			
Time	Session	Objective	Process/Notes
5 mins	Set up prior to arrival of client	**To set the room or space up to best support the needs of the session.**	Prepare: • Table with two chairs side by side • LEGO® bricks - preferably a LEGO® Serious Play® Starter Kit • Clipboard, paper and pen for note-taking
5 mins	Skills Build - 1	**To become familiar with the bricks.**	**"Build a model of a tower"**
5 mins	Skills Build - 2	**To introduce the client to LEGO® Serious Play** **To build two skills, develop story telling and understand use of metaphors.**	Explain the principles of LEGO® Serious Play® and facilitate a simple Skills Build. **"Take 3-4 bricks and build the first thing that comes to your mind."** "Now tell a story about what you just built." If the client has not used any metaphors, take turns to describe the model using the 'Explain This!' cards (page 111).
10 mins	Building future goals	**To identify and explore goals.**	Now ask: **"Build a model or models to show your own important personal or professional goal(s)"** - 4 mins Ask the client to tell the story of their model and ask questions about it.

Facilitation notes *narrative*

Before diving into the goal setting session, have a brief discussion with your client to establish the nature of the goal setting. Assess if the goal setting is personal, professional or both..

The Skills Build is like that for large groups (read Part 4), and it can be handy to have the A3 boards to explain the LEGO® Serious Play® process and etiquette.

Metaphors are an important skill for the client to develop. It frees them from feeling the need to build technically sophisticated models and allows them to communicate complex ideas with simple or even single bricks.

To explain, you could take a white 2x2 stud brick and suggest that you could use this brick to express a polar bear (see page 93), democracy (equal size studs), good health or cake!

You could also both play the 'Explain-this!' game that is explained in detail on page 111.

Overarching Objective Set goals and develop an action plan			
Time	Session	Objective	Process/Notes
10 mins	Current reality	**To identify the current reality of the client.**	"Build a model, or models, to show your current situation or reality in relation to your goal." Once the build is finalised, reflect upon the differences between the current reality and the goal.
5 mins	Blocks	**To identify blocks that may prevent the achievement of these goals.**	Ask the client to build 'roadblocks' "Build a model to show what might be stopping you from achieving your goal." Reflect on the model with the client.
5 mins	Action plan	**To plan actions.**	Ask the client to build a simple action plan to get past the roadblocks: "Now build your actions that will lead you past the most difficult roadblocks."
5 mins	Reflection	**To reflect on insights or meaning.**	Consider showing the client your notes
10 mins	Summarise and record	**To understand client feedback on the outcome of the session.**	Ask the client to reflect upon the value of the session. Invite the client to take photos of the models before they are broken up

Facilitation notes *narrative*

You might place the Goal Model at one end of the table and then ask the client to build a model or models to tell a story about the current reality of the clients world.

Ask the client to position the current reality model(s) in relation to the Goal Model. This landscape may reveal further data.

Invite the client to build a model or models with the bricks. These might represent external or internal factors (attitudes, mindsets etc.) or both. If needed, invite the client to be super honest. The builds might make the client feel vulnerable.

This is where the client can build an action plan of things they can do to overcome the blocks and step closer to achieving the goal.

It can be useful to have some sticky notes, so the client can briefly annotate the key ideas before photographing their models.

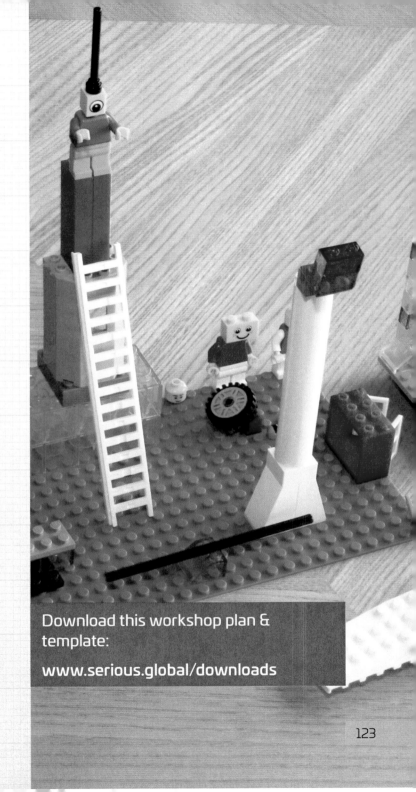

Download this workshop plan & template:

www.serious.global/downloads

Part 5.2

 **A Team Build Workshop**

Team Build

12 people, 4 hours

Thanks to Rita Fevereiro and the team at FutureLearn for allowing us to share this case study.

Background

A difficult aspect of working in teams is communication. It can be hard to say what you think, or share your reality and the way you see the world. People also struggle to be open to hearing what others see, perceive or believe.

What is an effective team?

An effective team

- Is bound by shared and meaningful purpose
- Is focused on shared goals
- Operates with shared values
- Communicates fluently
- Has trust in each other
- Learns to improve constantly (through feedback).

Team building is an ongoing process that helps groups evolve into a cohesive unit.

When team members share expectations for accomplishing group tasks, trust and support one another and respect one another's individual differences, a healthy team culture grows.

Team building with LEGO Serious Play

- Builds trust
- Enhances openness
- Improves communication
- Respects differences
- Increases creativity
- Shares expectations for accomplishing group tasks.

Background

In this case study we show how a team used LEGO Serious Play to build trust, understand hidden strengths and give feedback to each other.

The workshop also helped them build a shared team vision, identify negative behaviours that they wished to move away from, and positive behaviours they wished to see more of.

The brief

Rita was unusually clear in her brief and provided a focused set of objectives she wanted the workshop to achieve. We agreed an overarching objective for the workshop:

To create a stronger team with a clear picture of our team vision and understand the positive and negative behaviours needed to realise our team vision.

The preparation

This objective was translated into a draft workshop plan in the form of a set of facilitation notes which are reproduced in full in the pages that follow. Rita and I reviewed the draft plan to ensure it fitted her expectations and we made minor adjustments to it.

This case study focuses on using LEGO Serious Play to improve communication, give feedback, create openness and build trust.

In this case study, we don't go into detail about the Vision and Behaviours components of the workshop, as those are covered in detail in Parts 5.4 and 5.5 of this book.

Often in the on-going process of team building, groups might start with a 2 hour LEGO Serious Play Workshop to learn the LEGO Serious Play skills and focus on building trust, opening communication and respecting differences.

Team vision, values and behaviours can follow in later workshops.

Room set up

It's wise to check the room to be booked **before** the workshop in person or online to make sure it is big enough and has the furniture you need. A LEGO Serious Play Workshop for 12 participants needs a room that 20-30 people might typically use. If you combine several tables, use tablecloths to ensure that bricks do not fall between them.

For a workshop of this scale and complexity, allow an hour to set up. Usually this involves moving tables and chairs from a classic board meeting set-up to a more intimate set-up with tables to create a main table for group work, a table with no chairs for Shared Model building and spare tables for bricks.

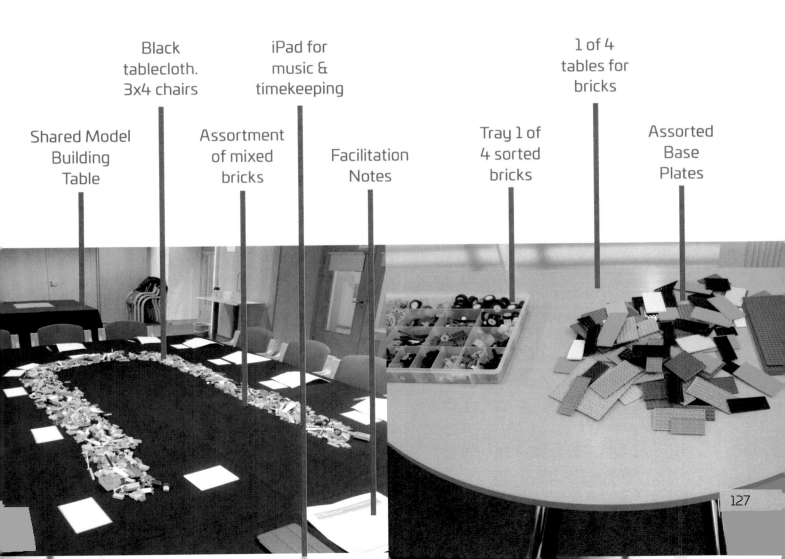

Black tablecloth. 3x4 chairs

iPad for music & timekeeping

1 of 4 tables for bricks

Shared Model Building Table

Assortment of mixed bricks

Facilitation Notes

Tray 1 of 4 sorted bricks

Assorted Base Plates

Overarching Objective **To create a stronger team with a clear picture of our team vision and to understand the positive and negative behaviours needed to realise our team vision.**			
Time	Session	Objective	Process/Notes
60 mins	Set up	**To get the room ready to support the needs of the participants and the workshop.**	Sean to set the room up to support the needs of the workshop. Set up to include: • Table for team to work on • 2-3 Tables for LEGO® bricks • Table for Shared and Final models, INCLUDING Feedback models • Video gear • Tripod, camera and boom mic for recording stories • Name badges • Music
5 mins	Welcome & objectives	**To clarify the workshop objectives.**	Rita + Head of Marketing to cover welcome & objectives. • Introduce Sean
5 mins	Workshop overview	**To give participants an understanding of the shape and flow of the workshop.**	Sean to give a brief overview of the workshop LEGO® Serious Play® Team Build Workshop Enjoy and find beneficial Respect the tables. Keep free of everything except bricks/gridcards Skills build.

Facilitation notes *narrative*

These notes were used in the workshop. The notes were refined based on three iterations between the client and facilitator before the workshop began.

Download these notes and use YOUR objectives and desired outcomes to edit the plan to suit your needs.

A short introduction from the project sponsor can be included (5 minutes is perfect) to thank participants for coming, state the objectives and introduce the facilitator.

Beware of long (anything over 10 minutes) monologues from the boss at the outset.

The message that long opening speeches give (in addition to the content) can be interpreted as: 'What the senior people think is more important than what participants think' and 'this is a top down, non-participatory meeting,' so 'being passive is OK.'

Of course this is the very opposite of participatory leadership.

Download this workshop plan & template:

www.serious.global/downloads

129

Overarching Objective To create a stronger team with a clear picture of our team vision and an understanding of positive and negative behaviours needed to realise our team vision.			
Time	Session	Objective	Process/Notes
40 mins	Skills Build	To give participants LEGO® Serious Play® skills (Technical, metaphor and story telling)	1. Technical - **Build a Tower** | 2 mins + 10 mins share Music – Snap out of it 2.. Metaphors - **Explain this!** | 30 seconds + 10 mins share 3. Story telling - **Build a model of your Dream Holiday** | 2 mins + 10 mins share Music – Happy Windows Kits. Then bag up Boards: Etiquette, Core Process
10 mins	Effective teams	To clarify the workshop objectives	HANDOUT: Gridcard What are two key qualities of effective teams? Bullet point a couple of words, not a paragraph. What key thing is needed to build an effective team? Reflection on Teams: Are those the qualities and things needed to build effective teams?

Facilitation notes *narrative*

A classic LEGO® Serious Play® Skills Build. See Part 4 for a detailed plan about how to facilitate this component.

Allow more time than this in your first workshops.

During each round of sharing, bring participant attention back to the core ideas in the models they build.

Use prompts like:

'Tell the story of the model.' 'Touch and point.' 'Listen with your eyes.' 'Be curious about what each others' models mean.'

Acknowledge participants who do these things well to try to develop these group habits. Watch for people who build models and don't use them to tell the story, and politely help them focus.

It can be helpful to use the A3 boards to remind participants of the Etiquette and Facilitation Fundamentals.

Participants during the skills build. Each was given a Windows Exploration Kit to use, but you could use any selection of bricks.

+ See 'The bricks - how to get them' in Part 3.

Overarching Objective **To create a stronger team with a clear picture of our team vision and understand the positive and negative behaviours needed to realise our team vision.**			
Time	Session	Objective	Process/Notes
30 mins	My identity	**To share with each other how we see ourselves at work today.** Build models of individual team members as they see themselves today	Introduce participants to the LEGO® Landscape & Identity kit **Build a model to show your core identity. Show who you are as you see yourself today** Think about your values, competencies and what really matters to you 5 mins build 10 mins share > Facilitator Instructions: Think of these models as solid thought. Like 3D prints of your mind. Imagination made tangible. Music – Snap out of it Share 1-2 mins each
15 mins	Break		

Facilitation notes *narrative*

The Landscape and Identity kit contains a wide range of bricks, from LEGO® DUPLO® bricks (which will connect to LEGO® when you know how), to technical bricks such as hinges, swivels, animals and insects, skeletons and gold bars.

It's worth a brief introduction to these bricks as well as offering technical support should people struggle to make the connections they want.

You could frame this task in the following way: 'How you see yourself might not be how others see you. Use this task to build a model to show who you really are at your core. Your core identity if you like.'

Take any questions for clarification before the build starts.

If you see anyone not building after 20 seconds, remind the group of the etiquette and to 'trust your hands.' Just start building.

Overarching Objective		
To create a stronger team with a clear picture of our team vision and to understand the positive and negative behaviours needed to realise our team vision.		

Time	Session	Objective	Process/Notes
20 mins	Johari Window 2 Trust	**To share more of ourselves with each other.** Use the Johari Window Model to share more of ourselves with each other (and build trust)	> Facilitator Instructions: SLIDE: For small groups use Johari Window A3 boards (see page 136 of this book) Introduce Johari Window Model Previous exercise helped you to show your public 'open room' Teams with high trust are more effective This exercise will help others to understand you better **Modify your model to show something that others don't know about you.** This does not have to be a deeply personal secret (but feel free!). It might be something you've just never got round to sharing Or perhaps something **you wish other team members might know about you to make you feel happier or better in this team** 3 min build + 10 mins share

Facilitation notes *narrative*

This exercise used the Johari Window concept. (If you are not familiar with this, read more on the web.) The A3 Johari Window overview boards are shown on the next pages.

The key idea is that teams with high trust are more effective. Each of the three 'knowing windows' is an opportunity to build trust.

Before the workshop, try the Johari build challenges yourself. Build models of your own public identity, then modify your model to show part of your hidden identity.

When asking people to share something of their 'hidden room' it is important to both give people permission to express hidden aspects of themselves **as well as making sure people feel safe and are not 'expected' to reveal things they would rather not.**

There are no right or wrong answers. Trust people to go as far as they wish to in their professional or personal lives.

By sharing more with others about ourselves, the Johari Window exercises help build trust in teams. Teams with greater trust are more effective.

135

Johari Window - Four Rooms

Download this A3 Board @ www.serious.global/downloads

First are the things you know about yourself and share

Others - know

Open 'Room'

My public self

Blind 'Room'

My blind spots

Then there's what others know about you, but you don't know about yourself

Next are the things you know about yourself, but choose not to share

Others - don't know

Hidden 'Room'

My hidden self

Unknown 'Room'

Unconscious self

Then the room of not knowing

Self - know   Self - don't know

Johari Window-Build Trust

Download this A3 Board @ www.serious.global/downloads

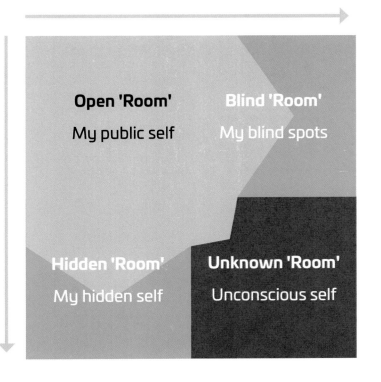

Ask - Constructive feedback increases self awareness

Tell -
Disclose
information
about
yourself

Open 'Room'

My public self

Blind 'Room'

My blind spots

Hidden 'Room'

My hidden self

Unknown 'Room'

Unconscious self

We can use the Johari window to help build trust in teams.

Teams with high trust are more effective.

The more others understand you,

the more you open up to each other,

the more rapport and trust is developed.

As a result relationships strengthen.

Overarching Objective			
To create a stronger team with a clear picture of our team vision and understand the positive and negative behaviours needed to realise our team vision.			
Time	Session	Objective	Process/Notes
40 mins	Johari Window – how others see you	**To understand how others see us** **Then offer feedback to each other about how others in the team see us.**	The 'blind' room SLIDE: For small groups use Johari Window A3 boards. **Please build a model to show a key professional strength of… (the name of the person on the slip of paper)** 4 min build + 10 mins share + 10 mins handover This might be something you think they are not aware of, or could be more fully aware of. Or a strength they have that they underplay. Be generous - evoke the best (but not the really obvious) Summarise this person's strengths in 3 or 4 words on a gridcard. • Share • Take Photos • Reflections

Facilitation notes *narrative*

Using the Johari Window to give feedback.

The task was framed as positive feedback with the question asked being to 'build a model to show a professional strength of...' but we could have also offered feedback on perceptions of learning edges or development needs. Decide before the workshop who is offering feedback to whom.

It can be good to ask a person who is not a close workmate (or does not get on!) to give positive feedback. Prepare small slips of paper like this:

> John, please build a model to show a leadership strength that Karen has.

Ask everyone to keep the names secret as they build and share the stories of the models.

After all models have been shared, ask each person in turn to say who the model was of and invite the builder to give the model to the person who is receiving feedback. Keep the models if you want to photograph people with them later.

This participant was seen by a member of his team as being a creative, instrumental lynchpin. Respect.

Team Build

The purpose of this part of the book was to enable you to understand how a Team Build component of a LEGO Serious Play Workshop was facilitated.

In this workshop, after we had completed the team building exercises, the group went on to consider a vision for their team, as well as to identify the positive and negative behaviours required to achieve the vision.

In order to observe the progression, a shortened version of the facilitation notes for the remainder of the workshop are shown on page 141.

Shared Vision

Part 5.4 of this book covers a Shared Vision in a different workshop if you'd like to see that application in action.

Values and Behaviours

Part 5.5 of this book covers Values and Behaviours in a different workshop if you'd like to see that application in action.

Next, you can read a clients reflections and learning having used LEGO Serious Play for the first time in her work setting.

This participant was seen by a member of her team as having a cool head under pressure. Nice.

Overarching Objective
To create a stronger team with a clear picture of our team vision and understand the positive and negative behaviours needed to realise our team vision.

Time	Session	Objective	Process/Notes
20 mins	Team vision	To build a model of a vision the team has for itself in 12 months.	See Part 5.4 of this book for a Shared Vision case study
30 mins	Shared Model	To build a Shared Model of a vision the team has for itself in 12 months.	See Part 5.4 of this book for a Shared Vision case study
40 mins	Positive and negative behaviours	To identify the behaviours that will help realise the vision.	See Part 5.5 of this book for a Values and Behaviours case study
20 mins	Reflections and learning	To share triple loop learning from the workshop.	A reflect, write, share task on what participants have learnt during the workshop.
60 mins	Close		Photograph models.

Workshop outputs

Identity and feedback models, a shared
team vision and positive and negative
behaviour models.

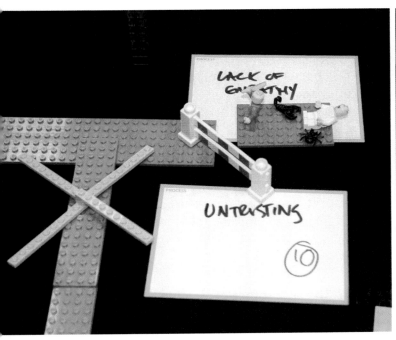

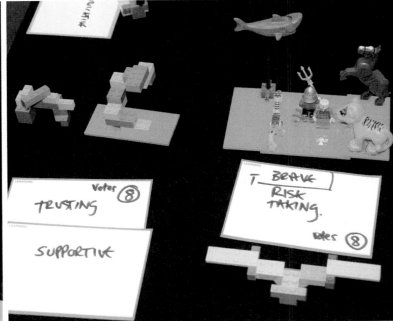

Workshop Learning

What I've learned about the power of LEGO Serious Play as an effective communication tool. By Rita Fevereiro

This has been reproduced from the article "The Workshop Client, written by Rita on LinkedIn Pulse. Read the full article http://bit.ly/Rita-Lego.

#1 Everyone builds and everyone shares

For every challenge or question, everyone needs to build a model using LEGO® bricks. Sometimes there will be specific instructions, others it's pretty much up to the person building the model. But the most important is that everyone builds something and shares what they've created.

#2 There are no wrong answers

No matter what you build, there is no right or wrong answer. It's your creation, your ideas and your view. Everything is valuable and relevant.

#3 Sharing is mandatory but only to a certain point

Everyone needs to explain the models they've built but they can reserve the right to only explain it to a certain extent. Especially if they've built something personal that they don't feel comfortable explaining in detail. I'm not sure if we were an odd team but everyone was open and willing to share more about themselves, which was both inspiring and fun.

#4 Creativity is enhanced by the use of metaphors

I was astonished by the creativity of the team's individual models. Not so much due to anyone's special expertise in building but because everyone was really engaged and used their imagination to explain concepts and thoughts that bricks alone wouldn't be able to reflect.

#5 The power of listening and speaking with your eyes and hands

We were always encouraged to explain each model with our hands and point to the different elements as we told its story.

This helped with bringing the story to life, but also made it much more powerful as others listened attentively and followed the model of the person sharing the story with their eyes as much as with their ears.

#6 The importance of building individually and together

I've enjoyed building my own models and seeing how far my creativity could go as much as I've enjoyed listening to everyone else's stories. I've learnt more about the personal and professional selves of each member of the team and that, in itself, was a good outcome. Building a shared model, a common vision that we all can look forward to, was by far the most enjoyable experience. It felt good as the team worked together and shared their concerns, aspirations and motivations.

We've built a shared model of what we want to achieve by 2017. It includes a wheel, a dynamic bridge, warriors, a tiger, an elephant, and much more. But of course, these are all metaphors :-).

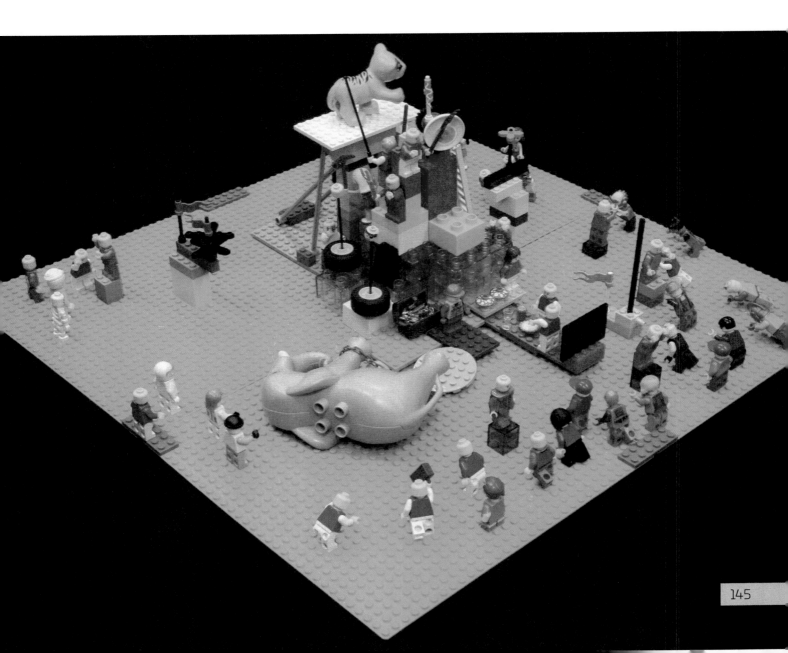

Part 5.3

 **An Ideas Workshop**

Ideas Workshop

12 people, 4 hours

Thanks to Karl Anton and the team at Telia for allowing us to share this case study.

Background

In this case study we show how a cross functional team at Telia used LEGO Serious Play to develop new service ideas for a new strategy in IPTV. IPTV is a television service delivered via internet.

Telia is a large international Telecommunications service provider. IPTV related services are one of the most important growth segments at Telia Telco. Karl Anton, the chief of TV division at Telia, asked Marko to facilitate an ideas workshop with the objective:

To create new product and service ideas for Telia TV.

Brainstorming with Bricks

Most of us have participated in brainstorming sessions and know the principles. Free your mind. Be open. Don't criticise. Keep the pace. The principles provide a safe environment to come up with lots of ideas. LEGO Serious Play is a good tool to help generate ideas.

The bricks create a playful mindset. The atmosphere is open and critique-free.

A model from the 'Invent a bicycle' Skills Build

A facilitator pacing through the tasks helps to achieve flow. Some builds use humour that, in turn, fuels creativity and fun.

LEGO Serious Play Ideas Workshops can take different forms. You can run your session with just a few people but the approach is so universal that, with proper skill and preparation, it can be scaled to larger groups. Be guided by three principles for this kind of workshop:

1. Pay attention to proper Skills Building

2. Keep the pace and flow

3. Make sure that all the ideas are captured.

Skills Building for ideation

Ideation relies on associative thinking. People need to be in a state of flow and therefore it is very important that they feel really comfortable with the bricks.

Never cut or rush the Skills Building of your Ideas Workshop.

The first skills building exercises are already familiar from the previous chapters of the book.

To put people in the right mindset for Ideas Workshops, however, the Skills Building also needs to fuel creativity.

We therefore suggest to also use a fourth Skills Building task: "Invent a bicycle." Read about this task in detail in the facilitation notes that follow.

Room set up

The bricks should be spread out in a random manner to support idea generation. This allows participants to rummage through bricks and build by quick association; whatever comes to their mind.

Using four tables is an advanced LEGO Serious Play technique. We suggest running your first LEGO Serious Play ideation session with 1 table and 4-6 participants.

Idea Builds at the corner of every table

Random bricks on all tables

Flipchart to record ideas

Facilitator table. Contains spare bricks, hand-outs, iPad, music & slideset

Food & drinks next door

149

Overarching objective: Create new product and service ideas for Telia TV focussing on four strategic direction areas.			
Time	Session	Objective	Process/Notes
Allow 60 mins	Set up	To set the room up to best support the needs of the session.	• Presentation slides • Clock/timer • Workbooks for every participant • Pens for every participant • Four tables, each with LEGO® bricks
5 mins	Welcome and Introduction	To set the scene for participants and introduce the facilitator.	Karl Anton to introduce the ideas day – inform about the recent successes on the market and the objective of the workshop.
40 mins	Introduction to LEGO® Serious Play®	To give participants LEGO® Serious Play® Skills.	Skills 1: **Build a Tower** (2 minutes to build). Sharing and reflection (8 minutes). Skills 2: Story: "Build myself" (1-minute build, 14 minutes for introductions). **Build a model of yourself using bricks and introduce your building to other participants, stressing who are you and what is important to you!** Skills 3: Metaphor: "Explain this!" Explain this! (1-minute build with just 5 bricks, 10 minutes for explanation.) Everybody gets to explain what their building means, e.g. "My TV Set," "Dream Television Service," "Our client," or "Future of telecoms" etc.

Facilitation notes *narrative*

Download and edit these notes, but use YOUR objective to edit the plan to suit your needs.

In this workshop Marko ran four tables concurrently. Managing concurrent tables is a more advanced skill. We strongly recommend you work with a single table until you have been trained or have successfully delivered this workshop a few times.

Use the A3 explainer boards to remind people of the etiquette and enhanced communication the process demands.

A LEGO® Serious Play® Skills Build. See Part 4 for a detailed plan about how to facilitate this component.

This Skills Build included two additional rounds within a story telling round - 'Build Myself" and "Invent a Bike" (described in detail overleaf). Allow more time than this in your first workshops.

Download this workshop plan & template:

www.serious.global/downloads

Overarching objective: Create new product and service ideas for Telia TV's four areas of strategic direction.			
Time	Session	Objective	Process/Notes
20 mins	Invent the bicycle	To deepen the skills and put the participants into the ideation flow.	Facilitator: **Build as many business ideas about bicycles as you can** Build individually Shout out your ideas Put the model in the centre of the table Build the next idea The team that has the most ideas wins! 10 minutes for building, 10 minutes for reflection of the ideas
20 mins	Build customer personas and their needs	To build customer personae for four client segments: 1) Business customers 2) Young customers 3) Y-generation customers 4) Elderly customers	Focused idea generation for client segments Each table select a segment group Individual build. **Create a persona and build his or her TV and entertainment needs and desires** 3 mins, then share stories of personae: Use the marker and write down the most important needs and desires of the customer personae to sticky notes

Facilitation notes *narrative*

Creative Thinking Skills Building exercise: "Invent a Bike"

This Skills Build is useful for ideas workshops, as it helps participants learn how to 'hand-storm' with short fast rounds of building.

Facilitator story: "You might have heard somebody say 'Don't invent a bicycle.'

Today we are going to do the opposite. You will have 10 minutes to invent and build as many **business ideas about bicycles** as you can. Everybody in your group builds individually. When you are done with your first building, just shout your business idea to the other members of your team, put it to the centre of the table and start working on the next idea. The team that has the most ideas wins!"

When participants start building, typically the first ideas are usually obvious, such as a bike shop, service, rental, racing and repairs. Then they become more playful, such as pizza delivery with bikes, cycling APPs, bicycle museums or a one-wheel bike circus.

And just before their building time is over, participants become really creative, developing ideas such as bikes for pets, for interior decoration, electricity from treadmill bikes, bike-shaped pizza knives, conference biking, bicycle parades in Santa costumes, and so on.

Participants will have lots of fun and enjoy the task. Once participants are in a state of flow, building a simple idea takes between 1 or 2 minutes. Therefore, a group of 3-5 participants is usually able to build around 8-16 funny ideas about bicycles.

Finish the exercise with a countdown from 5 to 1 and shout: "Now stop building." Ask participants to count their bicycle ideas and see who has got the most ideas. Thereafter ask them to reflect upon the ideas they had and show the results of the buildings to the rest of the group.

Overarching objective: Create new product and service ideas for Telia TV's four areas of strategic direction.			
Time	**Session**	**Objective**	**Process/Notes**
30 mins	Sharing personas and needs with the other tables	**To share ideas between groups.**	Share, listen and reflect People move between 4 tables and listen to the stories from other tables in relation to the four customer personas and their needs + Questions and reflections
15 mins	Break		
10 mins	Invent new business ideas	**To build product or service ideas to meet the needs of your personas.**	Facilitator: **Build ideas for products and services to meet the needs of your personas** Build individually Shout out your ideas Put the models in the centre of the table Build the next idea.
10 mins	Tables share and record	**To present the business ideas that were built for the needs of the 4 customer personas.**	On each table/segment group, participants share the business idea models After everyone has shared, invite participants to summarise their business idea model on a gridcard or sticky note. One per model.

Facilitation notes *narrative*

Frame the group share as an opportunity for participants to identify new needs for the personas they are working on.

Encourage participants to use the share as part of the idea generation process. The needs they identify here can be fuel for the "Ideas Session" next.

Before the key ideas session it is wise to hold a brief break as participants are usually tired.

A break helps to crystallize the stories and start the next brainstorming phase with renewed energy and a fresh start.

Observe participants. Some might get lost or stuck during the fast paced exercise.

Approach and support them quietly by asking friendly questions to help them move forward.

Participants during the session are to share between each table group.

Overarching objective: Create new product and service ideas for Telia TV's four areas of strategic direction.			
Time	Session	Objective	Process/Notes
30 mins	Sharing ideas with the other tables	To share between groups.	Participants move between 4 tables and listen to other stories about business ideas.
10 mins	Voting and selection	To choose the most useful and appropriate business ideas and solutions to meet the needs of customers.	Based on all ideas heard, the participants will walk around between the tables and "vote with flags" to choose the ideas they support the most Looking at results and reflection!
15 mins	Our action plan	The chosen ideas will be brought to life.	On tables, take the best ideas and write 30/60 day action plans. One per card of what actions or steps are needed to progress the ideas
20 mins	Sharing the personas and solutions with the other tables	To share between groups.	People move between 4 tables and listen to the action plan stories of others.
15 mins	Reflection & Learning	To share key learning from the workshop.	Gridcard and share

Facilitation notes *narrative*

Sometimes idea generation gets very creative and the quality and relevance of the ideas may vary.

You might suggest that the participants first decide upon criteria for voting. They might choose the ideas that are most closely aligned to the workshop objective.

Consider using a time box for action planning such as the next 30 or 60 days. Or suggest highly short time box actions such as "What will be the first thing that you will do during the next week?"

The reflection phase is frequently overlooked or occasionally even skipped when participants run out of time.

Asking participants what they have learnt about themselves, their team or the subject at hand is a great way to finish any meeting. The learning phase at the end of meetings can be one of the most important parts of the meeting!

Workshop Outputs

The workshop generated a lot of ideas! Of these ideas, Telia are happy for us to share the following.

Can you match the idea to the model?

- Sustainable TV Channel
- TV Gaming Solutions
- Cat Video Channel
- Fishing Web-Cam TV
- Partnership with Large Conglomerate
- Soap Opera Channel
- Ultra Wide Screen TV with Award Winning Augmented Reality

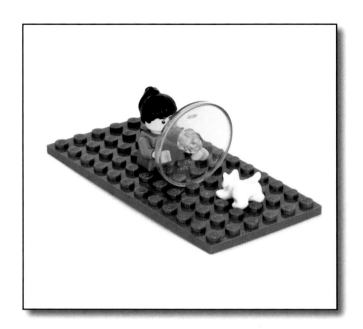

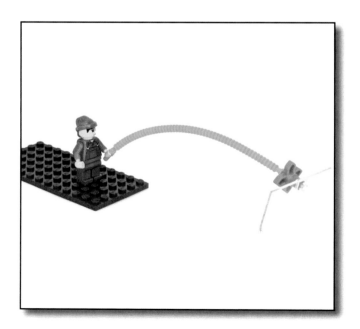

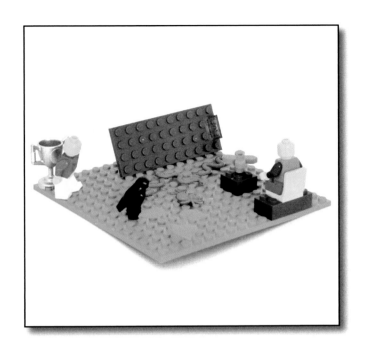

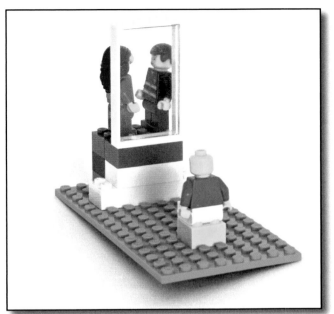

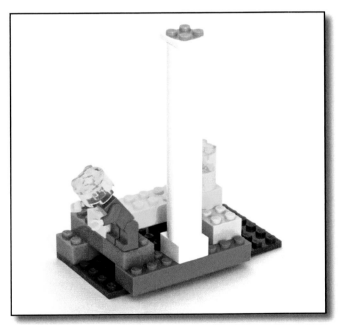

Workshop Outcomes

So, what happened next? 11 months later, our client Karl Anton, Chief of the Telia TV team reflects on the outcomes of the Ideation Workshop.

When we first contemplated a LEGO Serious Play workshop, our aim was to try something unconventional. A typical strategy might be 25 pages of Power Point slides that someone has drafted. We wanted to do something outside the box.

The LEGO Serious Play session with Marko was one the most extraordinary workshops that we have had at Telia.

The most unexpected aspect was getting to know our team members from a different perspective. We have some colleagues who are mostly doing technical or administrative work. I was positively surprised that everybody came up with so many creative ideas.

Our day-to-day jobs don't give all of us much opportunity to show our creative side.

LEGO Serious Play created an environment that opened everybody up in such an effective way.

Shortly after our LEGO Serious Play workshop we organised a follow-up event where we visited start-ups and learned how they put their ideas into practice.

These two events together helped us develop our ideas into a strategy that included a clearly formulated roadmap on which services to focus on, and how to move ahead with them.

Our strategy therefore became wider and clearer than our previous strategies and interestingly, it now includes some playful elements.

My colleagues have discussed the workshop several times. If I had to select just one word that we have used the most, it would be "fun."

Even though we were doing serious work it didn't feel like work because LEGO Serious Play made us enjoy it.

Karl Anton.
Tallinn
October, 2016

Part 5.4

 **A Shared Vision Workshop**

Shared Vision

11 people. 2 hours.
(Part of a 6-hour workshop)

Thanks to Peter Brennan, Vice President of Hotel Operations and Performance Support Europe at InterContinental Hotels Group, for allowing us to share this case study.

Background

In this case study we show how a newly merged team used LEGO Serious Play, Build Level 2, to create a shared vision for the team they aspired to 'become famous' for.

Two teams become one

As part of the ongoing process of change, two teams at IHG had merged. This workshop was the first time the new team had worked together in the new arrangement.

The workshop was six hours in total and was designed in service of the following objective:

To establish a vibrant culture for the new Operations Support Division Team through agreeing the vision, values and behaviours of (what will become) our famously successful team.

This case study will focus on the two-hour shared vision element of the six-hour workshop.

163

Briefing and method selection

After the client had briefed the assignment, we clarified our understanding of the workshop objectives and offered two process options; one using LEGO Serious Play, the other using more traditional workshop tools.

The client thought that LEGO Serious Play was a good choice for this kind of workshop, so we completed the workshop design using the facilitation notes format that you'll see reproduced in the pages that follow.

A brief overview of shared model building

This case study is not intended to do more than illuminate the very basic principles of LEGO Serious Play Build Level 2: Shared Model Building.

Think of this section as a 'peek under the bonnet' rather than 'a set of full engineering drawings.'

Our hope is that you'll learn enough about Shared Model Building to want to know more. This facilitation skill is best learnt through doing.

One way of organising the smaller bricks. The containers (bought at a DIY store) have snap close lids and are more portable than the orange trays LEGO® provides with the Landscape and Identity kit.

Room set up and kit

Check the room is big enough

Prior to the workshop, check that the intended room is big enough for the activities. Ideally it would be best to do a site visit, review a floor plan or observe photos of the room online.

Read about what can happen when a room is too small in Part 6, page 229.

Move the furniture - create zones

Allow an hour to set the room up. This mainly involves moving tables and chairs from a board meeting set up to create three different zones.

Zone 1: Gear

Spare tables for bricks and other workshop equipment such as pens, cameras and sticky notes.

Zone 2: Group Work

You'll want tables with chairs for group work, individual model building and sharing.

Zone 3: Shared Model Building

A table with no chairs for Shared Model Building. Shared Model Building is an active task that is best done standing up.

ProMeet Wallchart ▬
Table 1 for bricks ▬
Camera and tripod ▬
Facilitation notes and iPad ▬

Table 2 for building ▬
Bluetooth speaker for music ▬
Gridcards or sticky notes ▬

Table 3 for Shared Model Building ▬
Story telling stick (a LEGO® ladder) ▬
Shared Model ▬

Select the right bricks

For this workshop I used Windows Exploration kits for the Skills Build. Participants bagged these bricks into zip close bags after the Skills Build was complete.

A slightly enhanced Landscape and Identity kit was used for the vision and exercises that followed.

What's happening in the stop frame video?

Each of the planned activities begins at:

+ 3 seconds: Shared model building

+ 8 seconds: Telling the story of the model

+ 19 seconds: Scales of agreement

+ 20 seconds: Lunch

+ 24 seconds: Values

+ 33 seconds: Positive & negative behaviours

+ 53 seconds: Action planning

+ 65 seconds: Learning

This photo is taken from a video taken of the whole workshop. Watch a 75 second stop frame movie of the entire workshop:

http://bit.ly/seriouswork-vision

Overarching Objective
To create a stronger team with a clear picture of our team vision and understand the positive and negative behaviours needed to realise our team vision.

Time	Session	Objective	Process/Notes
60 mins	Set up	To get the room ready to support the needs of the participants and the workshop.	Sean to set the room up to support the needs of the workshop. Set up to include: • Wallchart on blank wall with task headers • Round or square table for team to work on • Tables for LEGO® bricks • Table for shared and final models • Video the day • Tripod, camera and boom mic for recording stories • Name badges
	Arrival		9:00 for 9:30 start
10 mins	Welcome & Objectives	To clarify the workshop objectives.	Peter to cover: • Welcome • Overarching workshop objective • Workshop overview (but NOT current reality) • Introduce Sean
10 mins	Famously successful teams	To give the workshop a participative and upbeat beginning.	Gridcard Task: **Complete the sentence. "The famously successful IHG ops support team I'd like to belong to would... " No wrong answers. Be honest** Share. Post to wallchart.

Facilitation notes *narrative*

The facilitation notes that were used in the workshop had been refined between the facilitator and client through nine iterations. You may download the notes and adapt them to your needs.

Feel free to download and use these notes as a basis to work from, but use your objectives and customise the plan to suit the needs of your workshop.

PROCESS

Please complete the sentence
The 'famously successful' IHG ops support team I'd like to belong to would...

SUPPORT EACHOTHER
OPENLY & HONESTLY

This workshop began with a simple 'Think, write, share' warm up task to get everyone thinking about the workshop question and to normalise an equal and participative workshop culture.

Download this workshop plan & template:

www.serious.global/downloads

169

Overarching Objective
To create a stronger team with a clear picture of our team vision and understand the positive and negative behaviours needed to realise our team vision.

Time	Session	Objective	Process/Notes
10 mins	Current reality	To establish the facts about the current reality that the new ops teams must work with.	Peter to share pre-prepared gridcards.
50 mins	LEGO® Serious Play® Skills Build	To give participants three LEGO® Serious Play® skills.	A standard Skills Build - see Part 4 of this book for detailed instructions.
50 mins	Individual Visions leading to Shared Vision Define what Operations Support will be famous for (our vision)	To create a Shared Vision for the Operations Support Division. Vision definition for workshop: Vision for our team in 12 months time. A desirable and appealing picture of a future state.	**Task Frame:** It's June 2016. Your team has made the cover of Fast Company **Task 1: Working Alone** **Build a model to show what your team is famous for. What will you have done to become famous? Make your model illustrate the nature of that success using metaphors)** Music **When complete, write the headline of your cover story on a gridcard** **Task 2: Share** Everyone to share the story of their models Encourage active listening.

Facilitation notes *narrative*

After the skills build, the Window Kits were bagged up and put away. Sean then introduced participants to the Landscape and Identity bricks that had been set out on a separate table.

The task was framed using an innovation game: 'Cover Story.' Participants were asked to imagine that in 12 months time, their team had made the cover of a famous magazine.

Then, working alone, they were asked to use the bricks to build models of what their team had become famous for.

Four minutes were given to build. Music helps people concentrate and encourages people not to have discussions at this point in the process.

PROCESS

Congratulations! Your team is the Fast Company cover story! Please write a magazine headline to summarise the story your LEGO model.

OPS SUP. GOES GREEN USING DATA & LEVERAGING DIVERSITY... AND IT'S GOING TO STICK!

I asked participants to write a cover story headline to summarise their model.

Use the A3 explainer boards to remind people of the etiquette and enhanced communication that the process demands.

Overarching Objective To create a stronger team with a clear picture of our team vision and understand the positive and negative behaviours needed to realise our team vision.			
Time	Session	Objective	Process/Notes
60 mins	Shared Vision Define what Operations Support will be famous for (our vision)	**To create a Shared Vision for the Operations Support Division.** This exercise will create a single shared model to describe what the Operations Support Division team aspires to become famous for in 12/18 months time. It will be your Shared Vision for your team The scales of agreement will allow us to record and understand just how much agreement there is on this vision. They also help to understand questions or reservations people have about the shared vision	**Task 3: Flag the part of your individual model that's most important** (2 mins) **Task 4: Build a Shared Model of what your team will be famous for in 12 months time** (15 mins) **Music – Nigel Stanford** **Task 5:** (Video) Ask at least 4 people to tell the story of the Shared Vision. Video record each round. **Task 6:** Scale of agreement on Shared Vision 1. All: Select a position on the scale of agreement 2. Write gridcard (alone) 3. Plus key question/concern 4. Share (1 gridcard rule) and post Photograph scale of agreement and model.

Facilitation notes *narrative*

Shared Model Building – in brief

Build Level 2: Shared Model Building could be the subject of a few chapters or an entire book. Facilitating this process is best learnt through doing, but the headline process looks like this:

Task 4: Build the Shared Model

After everyone has shared their individual models, they are asked to place a LEGO® flag on the most important part or message of their model. The flagged part of individual models must be represented on the shared model. If it weren't then it would be hard for that individual to say that they share the final model. (You can see green flags in the photo on the next page.)

Next, invite the group to move to the Shared Model building table (without chairs). In the centre of the table should be a large blank baseplate. This is what the Shared Model will be built on.

Ask people to recap on the flagged parts of their models so everyone understands the collective key ideas. Then invite participants to build a Shared Model using the individual models as the source of ideas and bricks.

This process is best mediated through the models, rather than debate. After you invite a group to build a Shared Model, encourage them to move individual models or parts of models to the big baseplate and start to discuss why they have placed the ideas/models where they have.

Make it OK for people to move each others models around the big baseplate as they describe the meaning and story that is emerging. In larger groups of 8+, beware of several conversations and constructions happening concurrently. If this happens ask the group to have one conversation or people will lose the meaning of the part they are not involved with.

After about 15 minutes, a model that is beginning to look complete usually emerges.

Mid-way through building the Shared Model. Seeing all eyes on the models is a good sign that the conversation is being mediated through the models using the Enhanced Communication techniques.

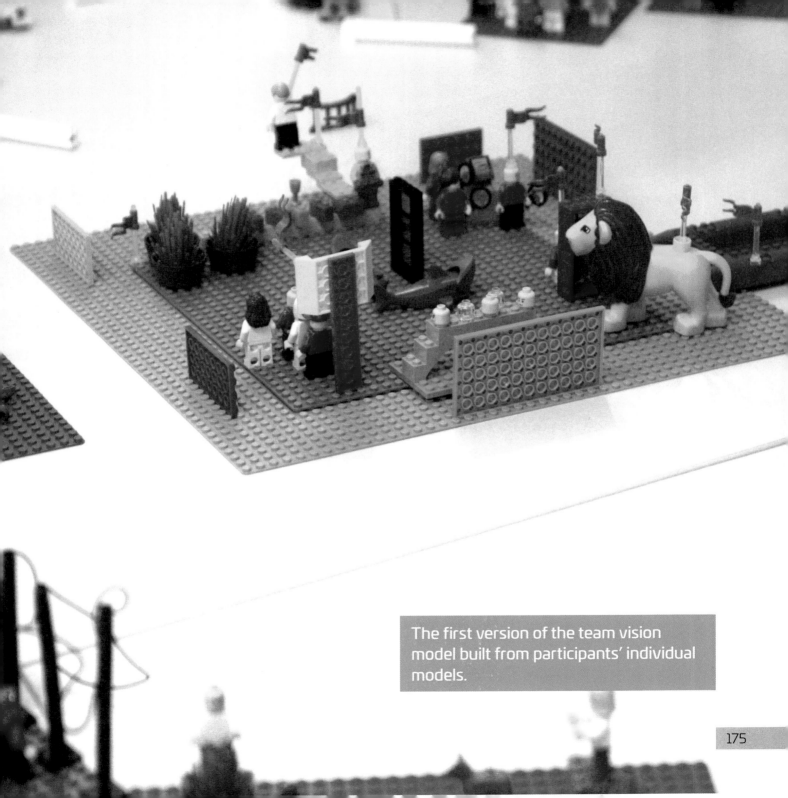

The first version of the team vision model built from participants' individual models.

A still from one of seven videos recorded during the Shared Model story telling. This participant is telling the story of the model as they understand it. Others are listening for common and different interpretations.

IHG Operations Support Team Workshop: Shared Model - Round 2

2:15 / 2:54

Facilitation notes *narrative*

Task 5: Telling the story and getting to common meaning

It doesn't matter if the Shared Model exercise feels incomplete before you move to this next stage.

Now invite one participant to tell the story associated with **every part** of the Shared Model. Ask them to **use a pointer**, in this case a LEGO® ladder, to help them focus on the model's story (not one in their mind) and tell the story of every part of the model.

Remind them there are no right or wrong answers, just different interpretations.

Suggest other participants **actively listen** because any of them might be taking the next turn. Usually it's a good idea to video this process, and there are several techniques to do this (see Part 6 for more hints). It's a good idea to remind everyone this is being recorded to keep background noise and chat down.

After the first person has finished, invite another to tell the story. Suggest it's not a memory game; they don't have to tell the story they just heard, but tell the story of the model as they understand it.

After they have finished, ask what differences people hear between the two stories. Use the differences to ask the group which meaning they share. Repeat this process and invite the group to amend the model as they go until a common understanding emerges.

In this example seven of the eleven participants told the story and recorded videos. The model was refined as they went. You can see the final model on page 180.

Task 6: Scales of agreement

We used another (non LEGO®) process called the 'Scales of Agreement' to understand individuals' key questions, reservations or concerns about the shared vision.

Read about this brilliant tool on the ProMeet blog: http://bit.ly/ProMeet-SoA

Vision Shared

The purpose of this part of the book was to enable you to understand how the shared vision component of a LEGO Serious Play workshop was facilitated.

This workshop continued to also consider values and behaviours. To illustrate what followed, page 179 provides a shortened version of the facilitation notes for the remainder of the workshop.

The Values and Behaviours Workshop

Part 5.5 of this book covers values and behaviours in a different workshop if you'd like to see that application in action.

At the end of the workshop, after the participants leave, carefully photograph all models before you pack up. Once they have been broken up, they are gone forever.

Of course the outcome you mostly want to create is ideas firmly lodged in peoples' minds that don't need photographic reminders.

Simple, powerful images, however, like the 'DON'T PUT UP BARRIERS', model are great reminders of the negative behaviours the team said it didn't want.

Time	Session	Objective	Process/Notes
Overarching Objective To create a stronger team with a clear picture of our team vision and understand the positive and negative behaviours needed to realise our team vision.			
45 mins	Lunch		
30 mins	Values	**To identify the key values needed to deliver the vision.**	See Part 5.5 of this book to see a values and behaviours case study
30 mins	Positive behaviours	**To identify the behaviours that will help realise the vision.**	See Part 5.5 of this book to see a values and behaviours case study
30 mins	Inhibiting behaviours	**To identify behaviours that will block the vision.**	See Part 5.5 of this book for a Values and Behaviours case study
15 mins	Break		
30 mins	Your vision, values and behaviours	**To identify key questions/reservations.**	Use the 'Scales of Agreement' to assess the level of agreement and identify remaining concerns.
45 mins	Action Planning	**To create individual action plans.**	Individual 100-day actions plans on gridcards. 10 mins alone then share
15 mins	Learning	**To reflect and learn.**	"Reflect, write and share" task. What have you learnt about belonging to this team today?

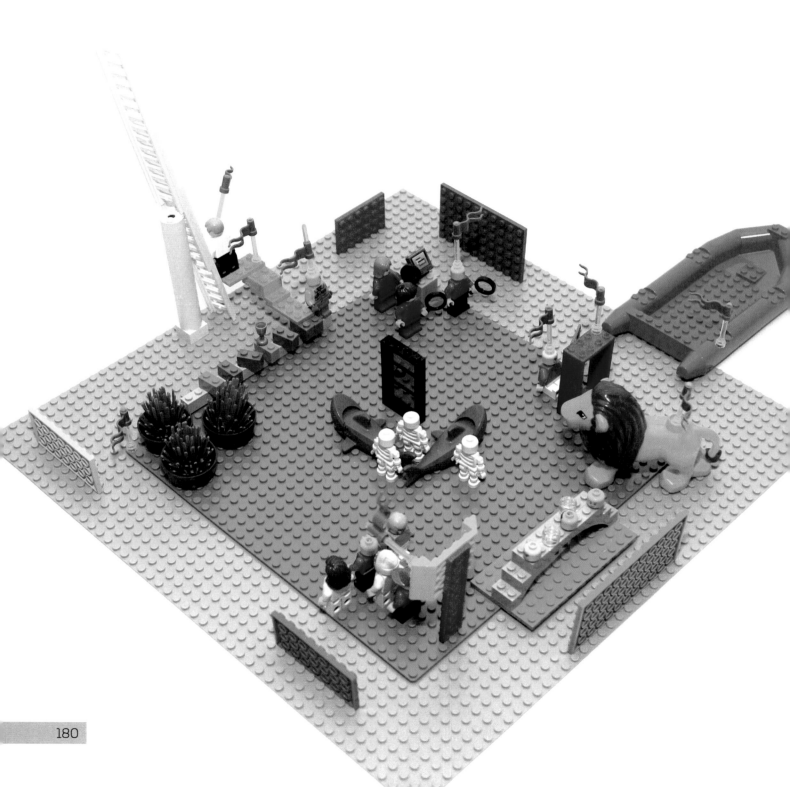

Photographing outputs

The workshop is over. Your client wants a record of what was built. It's not too difficult to take reasonable photos on site with a good camera, tripod and flash.

All the photos shown here were taken immediately after the workshop using either a white table top or a piece of flipchart taped to a wall.

Slightly overexpose the photos, use a narrow aperture (c f.18) and often do a quick tidy up in Photoshop or Aperture afterwards to adjust exposure, white balance and remove crumbs or flecks.

Team Vision Outputs

For someone who was not present it is hard to know what the vision model means. For the IHG Team, the shared vision they have for their team is...

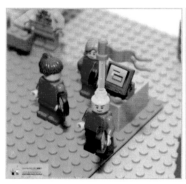

We're analytical and data driven...

We innovate and create solutions...

We take risks and know there is rescue available if needed...

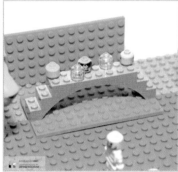

We build bridges in ops, with hotels and across IHG...

   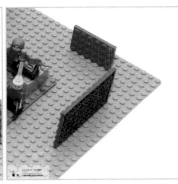

We understand our challenges and learn from previous experience...

We are all leaders and determine own our outcomes...

We cascade our messages and success as a team...

We place our brands at the heart of everything we do...

Workshop Outcomes

So, what happened next? 18 months after the workshop, the client Peter shared what happened afterwards.

Immediately after the workshop the team got back to the office with high energy and high engagement. We all had our '100-day actions plans' but then we thought about how to keep the ideas of the day alive. To help us with that we did three things:

Environmental reminders

We used the outputs of the workshop and made some posters to put in the office as environmental reminders.

This helped us remember what we did and helped us sustain what we'd learnt and agreed. It also reminded us of our behaviours and how we said we would act towards to each other.

LEGO® and play

We also bought some LEGO® sets as a reminder of how play is something that helps us to remember the ideas we created and shared; such as the team values we want and don't want. I think that element of play allowed the information and lessons to be sustained in the business and in the team.

If we had just gone to a traditional classroom training setting, even if we'd managed to get full engagement for the entire day, I'm not sure that those lessons would still be resonating with the team over 18 months later.

Encouraging values

The team had cards printed that showed the LEGO® model of the values we built on the front. When we see other people in the organisation exhibiting these values we write a congratulations note and send it.

These cards give staff reward and recognition. They say: **'I saw you do something that really lines up with our values, I just want to say thank you and well done.'**

Peter Brennan
Denham
October, 2016

VALUES

VALUES
BELIEF

VALUES
DETERMINATION & DRIVE

VALUES
TAKE RISKS

IHG OPERATIONS SUPPORT DIVISION
VISION

IHG used the workshop outputs and created postcards, mouse mats, wall posters and other assets to help keep the ideas alive in the minds of team members and spread the values through the wider organisation.

Part 5.5

Values & behaviours

Values & behaviours

22 people, 3.5 hours

Thanks to Jim Bowes, CEO of Manifesto Digital, and his team for allowing us to share this case study.

Background

Manifesto Digital are an award winning London based digital agency. They create change through combining ideas, design and technology. The outputs of their work are often apps and websites that aim to make people's lives better, easier and fairer.

Their CEO, Jim, had written their first 'business plan' some years previously during the start up phase of the business. He wisely thought it a good idea to involve the full team in a workshop to establish the values and behaviours they would need for their next period of growth.

We agreed an overarching objective as:

To build a stronger team with shared values and agreed behaviours: 'a new manifesto for Manifesto'.

I suggested that LEGO Serious Play would be a powerful tool to explore values and behaviours and also create a memorable set of tangible outputs.

Jim had come to a London LEGO Serious Play meetup group (see Part 7 for more about meetups), so had experienced the methods involved and

187

Sean's facilitation of it. He thought it could serve his team's needs well.

Objective driven workshop design

Exactly as described in Part 2 of this book, we used the 'objectives logic' and developed a set of workshop objectives outlining the actual tasks we would cover in the three and a half hours available.

Workshop Objectives:

To share workshop objectives

To assess current level of team development

To build basic LEGO Serious Play Skills

To share the 2017 Manifesto Vision with the team

To agree a lexicon for this workshop

To identify the core values of Manifesto

To identify the core positive behaviours Manifesto needs

To identify the core negative behaviours Manifesto does not need

To identify the Manifesto Simple Guiding Principles

To clarify what will happen next.

An input: Shared vision model

As you can see from the workshop objectives opposite, the workshop included a share of the Manifesto vision.

We'd convened a small workshop for the three directors just a few days before this full team session, during which the directors developed a Shared Vision Model.

The directors built a Shared Model and recorded videos of the Vision Model that were to be used during the full team workshop.

Brick selection

The warm up used Windows Kits that were given to every participant in a zip close bag. The values, behaviours and simple guiding principles used a Landscape and Identity kit.

Facilitation notes

These objectives translated into the facilitation notes below, which you can download at www. www.serious.global/downloads and adapt for your own use.

A note on group size

This workshop had 22 participants. Managing such a large group takes additional skill and experience. This plan will work well for smaller groups of 6-10 and be much easier to facilitate. Don't try this larger group size until you have developed excellent LEGO Serious Play facilitation skills!.

Overarching Objective
To create a stronger team with a clear picture of our team vision and understand the positive and negative behaviours needed to realise our team vision

Time	Session	Objective	Process/Notes
60 mins	Set Up	**To get the room ready to support the needs of the participants and the workshop.**	Sean to set the room up to support the needs of the workshop. Set up to include: • Screen/Computer/Speakers • 4 tables of 5/6 people • Tables for bricks • Tables for completed models
	Arrival		9:30 for 10:00 start
5 mins	Welcome & Objectives	**To share the workshop objectives.**	Jim to welcome Set the scene - run through objectives.
40 mins	LEGO® Serious Play® Skills Build	**To build basic LEGO® Serious Play® Skills** 22 x Windows kits Afterwards, bag up Windows kits and use Landscape & Identity kit A standard Skills Build - see Part 4 of this book for detailed instructions.	**1. Technical - Build a Tower** > Reflection: Use your model to tell your story Music – Snap out of it **2. Metaphors: Explain this! - use slides** > Reflection: You can make a brick mean anything. Technical 'fancy' builds are not needed. Listen with your eyes! **3. Story telling: Build a model of your dream holiday** > Reflection: Trust and think with your hands. Tell the story of the model, not the one in your head Music – Love Vibration

Facilitation notes *narrative*

These are the workshop notes.

Download and adapt to suit the objectives and desired outcomes of the group you are working with. Then develop the questions and the process.

Download this workshop plan & template:

www.serious.global/downloads

Mid-way through the LEGO® Serious Play® Skills Build - 'The Tower' using Windows Kits.

Participants were instructed to use a black baseplate and only green and orange bricks.

A limited selection of bricks helps illustrate the huge difference in possible solutions from just a few bricks.

Overarching Objective
To create a stronger team with a clear picture of our team vision and understand the positive and negative behaviours needed to realise our team vision

Time	Session	Objective	Process/Notes
10 mins	Manifesto Vision	**To share the 2017 Manifesto Vision with the team.**	CEO, Jim, to talk through LEGO® vision model - Use the film and model. Questions for Clarification.
5 mins	Lexicon	**To establish a Workshop Lexicon.** Behaviours, Values and Guiding Principles that will help Manifesto feel like Manifesto and achieve the vision.	Input. Use Projector + Slides **Behaviours** The way in which one acts or conducts oneself, especially towards others. **Values** Important and lasting beliefs or ideals shared by the members of a culture about what is good or bad and desirable or undesirable. Values have a major influence on a person's behaviour and attitude and serve as broad guidelines in all situations. **Simple Guiding Principles** Principles. A fundamental truth that serves as the foundation for a system of belief or precepts. A rule intended to regulate behaviour or thought, e.g. "the legal precept of being innocent until proven guilty," that guides an organisation throughout its life in all circumstances, irrespective of changes in its goals, strategies, type of work or the top management.

Facilitation notes *narrative*

Jim Bowes describes the vision for Manifesto produced by all three directors in a workshop a few days before the full team workshop.

Terms like 'vision,' 'strategy,' and 'values,' as well as less familiar terms like 'simple guiding principles' mean different things to different people.

It is usually a good idea (especially in workshops with many languages) to offer a working definition for the purpose of the workshop.

In this case the definitions were projected and questions for clarification taken and answered before the team were asked to build models of their ideas.

Overarching Objective			
To create a stronger team with a clear picture of our team vision and understand the positive and negative behaviours needed to realise our team vision			
Time	Session	Objective	Process/Notes
25 mins	Values	**To identify the core values of Manifesto.**	Work Alone. **Build a model of a core value that Manifesto needs to achieve its vision** Share: Form two groups of 10 people Individuals to share. Then ask group to vote, aim to get top 5 values plus a further supporting 5.
40 mins	Positive Behaviours	**To identify the core positive behaviours Manifesto needs.**	Half the group on positive, half on negative Work Alone: **Build a model of a core positive behaviour that you think Manifesto needs to achieve its vision** Vote
40 mins	Negative Behaviours	**To identify the core negative behaviours that Manifesto does not need.**	Work Alone: **Build a model of a core negative behaviour that you think Manifesto does not need** Identify a real negative behaviour that you have seen, experienced or personally performed in the last week or month Vote

Facilitation notes *narrative*

With larger groups use a projector for the build questions and a countdown clock.

This ensures everyone can read and understand the build question and has a sense of how much time they have for the task.

In large groups you will not have the time for all people to share in one big group. Divide large groups up into manageable sizes and ask each group to vote to identify the most popular ideas. Then share popular ideas in the large group.

With 22 participants, split the room into two groups, half work on positive behaviours, the other on negative. Invite participants to self organise into two groups based on their affinity to the build topic.

All participants voted on both sets of models and individuals had the opportunity to suggest behaviours they thought were missing.

Build a model of a core value Manifesto needs to achieve its vision

03 :00

Important and lasting beliefs or ideals shared by the members of a culture about what is good or bad and desirable or undesirable. Values have major influence on a person's behaviour and attitude and serve as broad guidelines in all situations.

Build a model of a core positive behaviour you think Manifesto needs to achieve its vision

Build a model of a core negative behaviour you think Manifesto does not need

03 :00

The way in which one acts or conducts oneself, especially towards others

Download the slides:

www.serious.global/downloads

During the workshop we opted to share the values as one big group (not 4 small groups as planned).

Always facilitate the people, not the process. If your carefully prepared plan is not what the group needs in that moment, adjust the process and facilitate what the group needs, not what you have planned.

Participants voting for the values and behaviours. Each participant has three bricks and three votes.

Overarching Objective
To create a stronger team with a clear picture of our team vision and understand the positive and negative behaviours needed to realise our team vision

Time	Session	Objective	Process/Notes
25 mins	Simple Guiding Principles (SGP)	**To identify the Manifesto Simple Guiding Principles.**	This is the big one. Using everything said so far, build a model to represent a SGP that you and others can use as a 'North Star' A SGP is NOT a rule. e.g. "If/Then…" A SGP is NOT a single word value e.g. Trust It's more like a 'boid' than a rule. (Boids are an artificial life program developed by Craig Reynolds in 1986, which simulates the flocking behaviour of birds https://en.wikipedia.org/wiki/Boids) "Steer to avoid crowding local flock-mates" is a good SGP for a bird in a flock. The key to SGP's is to **under-specify** to allow autonomy for a context-dependent reaction to every situation. Build alone: **Build a model of a Manifesto Simple Guiding Principle** Share in big group - then Vote.
5 mins	What Next?	**To clarify what next.**	Jim.
60 mins	Lunch	**Photograph models.**	

Facilitation notes *narrative*

This photo shows the Simple Guiding Principles after being shared by all participants.

Note that every model had been summarised on a gridcard by Sean, who had checked if his summary words were an accurate synthesis of the meaning.

Also note the bricks on the cards. Each brick is a vote. 'Get out of your comfort zone' got 8 votes and was selected to be one of the Simple Guiding Principles.

Workshop Outputs

Simple Guiding Principles

These models were photographed on a piece of flipchart taped to a wall. A touch of post production creates useful and memorable workshop outputs.

MANIFESTO GUIDING PRINCIPLE

HELP PEOPLE TO SEE SOMETHING

DIFFERENT

MANIFESTO GUIDING PRINCIPLE

GET OUT OF YOUR

COMFORT ZONE

Workshop Outputs

Values

These images show the values Manifesto Digital selected as those being core to achieving its vision and developing the culture the staff wanted.

MANIFESTO VALUES

EFFICIENCY

THROUGH SIMPLICITY

MANIFESTO VALUES

COLLABORATE

TO CREATE GREAT WORK

Workshop Outputs

Positive behaviours

These images show the positive behaviours the team wanted to encourage, recognise and reward.

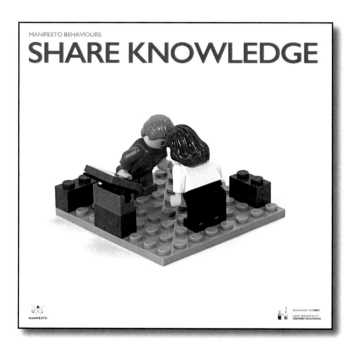

BE FREE TO CREATE

HAVE FUN

Workshop Outcomes

So, what happened next? This workshop took place in August, 2015. A year later, Manifesto CEO Jim Bowes describes what happened after the workshop.

Growing organisations move forwards and things change. Sometimes quickly! Our values and behaviours workshop took place during a period of rapid expansion and growth.

A few months after the workshop, we merged with another creative agency.

By December 2015, our team had grown by another 12 people, which meant a third of the new bigger team had not taken part in defining our behaviours and values.

We then had the challenge of creating a combined proposition for the merged agency.

Sean suggested we take the outputs and make a simple set of brand values. So with the new larger team we developed a new set of values:

1. **Collaboration:** Be forward and share knowledge; don't wait until you're asked.

2. **Innovation:** Help people to see something different. We strive for efficiency through simplicity.

3. **Excellence:** Be committed to always learning new things and using that knowledge to drive positive change.

4. **Change:** Never stand still. Keep your eyes open and spot opportunities before they arise. Don't be afraid to question; challenge yourself and others.

If you compare these with the LEGO® workshop outputs, you can see the DNA of the LEGO Serious Play Workshop ideas in our new brand values.

New Brand Values

These new brand values are at the heart of everything we do.

We use them as part of our induction manual for new staff (see opposite) and we use them to communicate everything we do on our website.

The LEGO Serious Play Workshop really helped us develop our new service and develop a more creative public-facing brand.

The LEGO® Workshop has even become part of our company history on our timeline of key events that shaped who we've become today.

Jim Bowes.
London
October, 2016

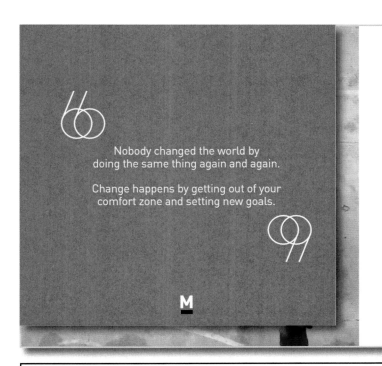

66

Nobody changed the world by
doing the same thing again and again.

Change happens by getting out of your
comfort zone and setting new goals.

99

M

HEY MARK,
WELCOME!
WE'RE REALLY
EXCITED TO HAVE A NEW
CREATIVE DIRECTOR
ON BOARD!

You've joined a brilliant team of creatives and technologists
who just love to collaborate to change the world for the better.
We cant wait to see how you'll help us achieve our goals.

We have four values that guide what we stand for.
Let us introduce them to you...

OUR BRAND

We're an agency with a brave name and a
bold, brave brand to match. Our brand is how
we present ourselves to the world and how
Manifesto is perceived; the thread that runs
through everything we do.

From how we talk to our clients to the products we develop for them, our brand
reflects our culture and values, and is present in the way we interact with anyone
on behalf of Manifesto.

Our tone of voice is authoritative without being condescending; fun without being
flippant; knowledgeable without being pompous.

You will have access to our full brand guidelines which set out who we are, how we
talk and what we look like. Become familiar with them to keep our communications
consistent and our brand working as hard as it can for us all.

M

Part 6

Practical tips

The objective of this chapter is to offer you practical tips to help you understand how brilliantly LEGO® Serious Play® Workshops are run.

Learn from respected peers

We invited respected LEGO Serious Play Facilitators from around the world to share their stories to emphasise the ideas in this book.

Camilla Nørgaard Jensen
USA/Denmark

Dieter Reuther
USA

Kristina Nyzell
Sweden

Mercedes Hoss
Germany

Kim Pong Lim
Singapore

Patrizia Bertini
Italy

Eli de Friend
Switzerland

Maria Stashenko
Russia

Oliver Knapman
China

Camilla Nørgaard Jensen

@CamillaJensen

Specialties:
Wicked Problems
Science Communication
Design Thinking

Scholar of Serious Play

I use LEGO® Serious Play® to facilitate cross-disciplinary communication on wicked problems. For my PhD research I applied LEGO Serious Play to deliver a nano-ethics curriculum at Arizona State University.

During class, my students used LEGO Serious Play to share their knowledge and values related to the implications and applications of nanomaterials. In addition to increased topic understanding, students reported that using LEGO Serious Play incited creativity and improved communication, due to the playful nature and because "you physically put your ideas on the table."

Even when struggling to combine their perspectives into a shared model, teams described these challenges as "fun frustration" that led them to be creative and think of stories that effectively conveyed their multifaceted considerations. Additionally, they felt they knew their fellow students in this class better than peers they had spent a full semester with in other classes.

My key takeaways from the experience

Participants must build skills to become fluent in self-expression through models and metaphors, especially on complex topics. I dedicated the first of the four workshops to Skill Building.

Large groups must be subdivided into smaller tables. I divided my twenty students into four teams of five participants each. For research purposes, ethnographic observers were assigned to each table, but they also served as my extension, clarifying prompts and signalling to me when their team was ready to move on.

LEGO® is designed to make noise when it's shuffled. It's part of the appeal, but in a large room it can interfere with discussion. Seek out a venue with good acoustics and use tablecloths to dampen noise whenever facilitating more than one table at a time.

When you end your workshop with a debrief exercise participants take mental inventory of the experience. One way to prompt reflection is to ask them to write out what "squared" with them (#square), three things that stood out to them (#triangle), and something that is still "circling" for them (#circle).

I use Twitter for this. It enables a public exchange of reflections to everybody's benefit. If something is unclear to one person it is probably unclear to others too. In consecutive workshops, the written reflections provide continuity, e.g. at the beginning of the next workshop I will clarify what they reported had been circling for them.

Eli de Friend

in defriend

Specialties:
Leadership Development
Executive Coaching
Strategy & Learning

Experienced LEGO® Serious Play® facilitator Eli de Friend shares ten wise suggestions.

Mastering the Flow

Preparation tips:

1. Understand your participants' profiles (educational level, professional experience, psychology, preferences and background).

2. Identify the "real" sponsor of the workshop. What types of relationships link the sponsor and participants (hierarchical, matrix, mutual interest, etc.)? Be clear who the client is.

3. Establish the "real" objectives of the workshop.

4. Always ask for more time than the client first offers, even if this requires offering to give some time for free. Up to a limit, the longer the participants have their hands on the bricks and are sharing ideas they care about, the more satisfied they will be.

5. Tailor the Skills Building to fit the participants' profile and theme of the workshop.

Facilitation tips:

6. Use visual as well as spoken instructions for announcing challenges, all the more so if either the facilitator and/or the participants are not working in their native tongue.

7. Check participants' understanding of the challenges and invite one participant to paraphrase the challenge to the others.

8. Know your facilitation roadmap and timing constraints. Occasionally, participants are so engaged in their conversation that they will not stop and insist that it is vital that they continue. You need to know what you could scrap that is still ahead and assess whether the current discussions are more critical to the main objective than the future steps.

This is where it is important to really know who the sponsor is and what the objectives are.

9. Respecting LEGO Serious Play etiquette doesn't prevent you from using tasteful humour, theatrics and audio-visual accompaniment. Get multi-sensorial!

10. While mixing methods may be useful from a conceptual perspective, and mixing materials may be fun from a participation perspective, for your own sake, never mix modelling clay of any sort with LEGO® bricks. NEVER.

We are still separating out bits of Play-Doh from some of our bricks 7 years after they were inadvertently united

Maria Shashenko

 fb.com/stashenko

Specialties:
Design Thinking
Human-Centred Design
Innovation Development

Three short cases. Nine big benefits

LEGO® Serious Play® is a great tool to visualise and model concepts such as strategies, ambitions, goals, business plans and visions. Here are three example applications and the benefits LEGO Serious Play brought in each case.

Case 1. Budget planning. Client: SAP CIS

Objective: To create a new budget aligned with innovation priorities and future vision.

LEGO Serious Play helped: Enliven routine budget planning practices through collaboration instead of individual work.

Release the creative minds of the participants to enable a fresh and innovative view on spending areas.

Reduce the time needed for budgeting by each department head.

Case 2. Education program development. Client: SAP CIS Education

Objective: To create new employee educational programs in companies applying SAP enterprise automation decisions for fostering learning effectiveness and efficiency.

LEGO Serious Play helped: Visualise existing hurdles and wicked problems in employee education.

Develop innovative ideas through fast and exciting 'brick-and-figures' collaborative work.

Create simple and easy-to-grasp models built to show 'new education processes,' 'new roles of the educator' and 'educational programs.' These models made communication of the ideas better and implementation easier.

Case 3. Project management office setup. Client: Aeroflot

Objective: To integrate IT and Business processes for more effective collaboration.

LEGO Serious Play helped: Explore and communicate painful business problems.

Break the barriers between IT and Business departments through representation of overlooked collaboration opportunities.

Create a new model of the office, which was more sustainable and effective.

I hope these brief stories show that LEGO Serious Play has few limits in applying to any area of business development, and also show that it brings real value in fostering innovation, creative thinking and team collaboration.

Dieter Reuther

🐦 @DieterReuther

Specialties:
Innovation
Design Thinking
Team Empowerment

My path, passion and commitment to LEGO® Serious Play®

As an engineer I believe in the power of tools and processes.

For every problem, engineers can find a technological solution. With this mindset, I implemented endless tools, systems and processes to foster creativity. I also sought to support the business aspect of creative project work during my 13 years in Design Operations at one of the leading US innovation and design consultancies.

These process and technology-based approaches, however, often only worked for a short time or were bypassed by the creative staff after an initial success. The struggle to maintain a certain level of creative chaos versus too much structure seemed to be the problem.

I had a hunch that all the efforts to throw processes and technology at our project teams were a lost battle. I therefore initiated a Six Sigma Project to get to the root of why some of our projects were successful and some were not.

Why did our clients fall in love with the outcome of some of our work while the project was on time and within its budget? Why did some projects require reworking, go overtime and lose money? Why were there so many frustrated staff?

The Six Sigma Program analysed 60 projects and scrutinized their schedule performance, budget adherence and rates of client return to either confirm or disregard initial assumptions. Was it the project size, the client size, the location of the client, or maybe the level of innovation? None of this seemed to have a significant impact.

The factor responsible for the outcome of our projects was the success of the pairing of the project leader with the project team and the individual team members. Some pairings worked well and others just disrupted the flow of projects and led to failure. The human aspect of our projects made them succeed or fail.

This insight that the human aspect of project work can play such a powerful role drove me to explore the power of LEGO Serious Play to help teams be more successful.

This play-based facilitation methodology helps uncover what is happening in the space between people and lay the groundwork for successful project outcomes. I love it when people forget their daily routines and dive into a safe environment of play and interact on a level playing field to rediscover their creative potential and solve complex problems.

Kim Pong Lim

in limkimpong

Specialties:
Culture Building
Leadership Coaching
Team Engagement

Building culture is at the heart of everything we do in Asia

We use LEGO® Serious Play® to help our clients articulate, breathe and live their culture; to engage their employees and allow everyone to achieve their best productivity.

We have often seen that the best plans, strategies and ideas are resisted and thwarted by entrenched enterprise cultures. Many organisations and teams sincerely want growth, innovation and change in their businesses. Yet many of them resist the very people, ways and ideas that could create those desired new growths, innovations and changes. What often stands in the way is the inability to articulate what is on our minds, listening to what others are saying or finding a way together to achieve shared goals.

LEGO Serious Play removes those inabilities. It facilitates rich and actionable conversations. It allows participants to face up to the complex realities of their work and relationships in a safe environment, eases them into describing difficult issues in greater detail and helps them focus and create outcomes that would otherwise have taken days or months.

The method is both the art and science of facilitating seriously rich and real conversations between people. We love using it to enable people to understand and be understood, to create openness to challenges and be challenged and to instil the belief that creativity is not the domain of some but the domain of all.

So far, all of our plays have been conducted in Asia and two things stand out: 1) Asians are generally less outspoken than their Western counterparts; 2) Showing respect for seniors and leaders is highly esteemed. Hence, in Asia, "giving face" is an age-old expectation and speaking one's mind in an environment where there are others more senior than you, is not.

It is in this space that LEGO Serious Play has its greatest role as a leveler, enabler and encourager for real and needed conversations. It draws out the unspoken thoughts and serves them with dignity and respect from everyone around the table.

Finally, here are five of my own personal "guiding principles" for conducting the facilitation:

1. Keep the play simple and uncomplicated.

2. Help clients learn and not just build.

3. Don't be afraid of silence. They are thinking.

4. Love the process. Trust the models.

5. Keep it moving.

Mercedes Hoss

🐦 @offtimeeu

Specialties:
Business Modelling
Future of Work
Cultural Intelligence

Turning my favourite childhood toy into a key tool for facilitating fertile and rewarding workshops.

I came across LEGO® Serious Play® by chance. Using LEGO® to resolve problems and to help identify the things that we already know but do not know that we know initially sounded too good to be true.

'It's a technique without content,' Robert Rasmussen would say at the beginning of our Facilitator Training. 'The facilitator asks a question, then the participants build the answer to that question with LEGO® bricks, using them metaphorically to add meaning.' After I had worked with Tim Clark to organise and co-facilitate Business Model You® workshops in Europe, I started combining the two methodologies.

A business model describes the process and rationale behind how (and in some cases, why) an organisation creates, delivers and captures value. The Business Model Canvas[7] is a strategic tool that allows you to describe, design, challenge, invent and pivot your business model.

By thinking of yourself as a one-person organisation, you can also use this tool to define and modify your own personal business model. It can help you to take advantage of your skills and aptitudes, to grow both personally and as a professional, and to reveal new, more satisfying career and life possibilities.

Personal business models are to do with who we are and how people see us as well as the as-yet untapped potential in us. Thus, creating them requires both initial self-knowledge and further self-reflection.

The business model canvas is usually completed using post-its to record our insights along the way. This helps us both to focus and to better understand what is key in why, what and how we do what we do, as well as how to take the next step in our career. I believe that adding a third dimension using LEGO® models to define areas that are more on the "soft side" could be useful in helping generate insights/a deeper connection with our emotional (YOU) side, and in understanding and defining a compelling and congruent value proposition that is based on a unique professional identity.

Taking time to consciously work on what is next for you in your career can be a tiresome process. Adding LEGO® to this process helps ease anxiety, put a smile on people´s faces, build new levels of trust and collaboration and enables you to feel and see 'a-ha' moments.

 7 https://strategyzer.com/

Patrizia Bertini

🐦 @legoviews

Specialties:
Innovation
Creativity & Co-creation
Systems Thinking

Inside the minds of others

Can you imagine how many stories are packed into the models participants build? Have you ever had the temptation to delve further and get more stories from the models?

I did. I wanted to explore the universe of meaning and stories hidden in those models and learn more about how people see the world. So I asked myself, what if I used the LEGO® Serious Play® approach for one-to-one interviews?

The first question I had to answer was: Which bricks can I use? The Window Exploration kit looked to be a good starting point; small enough, yet with sufficient metaphorical elements to boost storytelling. Then I found volunteers during the Occupy London movement.

As an ex-journalist, I had always felt the question and answer game was inadequate to really see the world through other people's eyes. Journalist questions often function as a filter.

Would LEGO Serious Play change this? It did. My first interviews were a revelation.

I asked participants to build the world as they saw it, keeping the questions open, unbiased, and broad to allow their point of view to emerge spontaneously.

I acted as a Socratic midwife, asking questions about their models, playing with them, moving and taking bricks away, challenging their points of view in a playful and non threatening way. It was not me leading the interview, but the bricks. I was careful in crafting the questions, avoiding leading clues, and tried to make sure participants were not biased by my point of view or expectations.

Participants shared their inner worlds and thoughts, feeling using the bricks. The bricks acted as a powerful medium and allowed people's universes to become stories and narratives.

Ever since, I have applied this maieutic approach in countless cases. I've tested it in political contexts such as Palestine and Israel, I have used it to explore complex concepts like colour, and I've talked to artists, activists, and business men through this approach.

The result is always the same. I can see the world through other people's eyes through their stories and words, and my role is just to guide them, through their models, to open up their universe to me in a journey we build together.

Oliver Knapman

🐦 @Oliver_LSP

Specialties:
Brand Identity
Change Management
Process Mapping

A useful lesson

This is a story about a workshop that created a team that understood themselves, their colleagues and their work better. It also created a very disappointed Human Resources Director.

The client was the Director of a purchasing department in a large multi-national company. Her team was undergoing a big structural change, making the transition from a collection of business units spread across the globe to a unified system.

We took great care to prepare the session. We managed expectations about the process and method, and used LEGO® in pre-meetings to gather requirements and share understanding of what we were going to do.

We agreed the session was to help the management team to rethink their position within this system and set out a new way of working that would carry them forward.

Exactly the type of scenario a LEGO® Serious Play® Workshop can make a positive impact on.

We designed a workshop to help identify 'guiding principles' and 'the spirit in which things are done.'

During the workshop, however, it became clear that the client HRD was becoming increasingly frustrated with her perception of 'the lack of concrete outcomes.'

It turned out that the client wanted us to augment participants' job descriptions with two lists; good behaviours and bad. Instead, we were facilitating a workshop to surface feelings, values and mindsets.

Extremely useful for the team, but not, it turned out, what the client wanted.

We took a few lessons from this experience.

It is vital that you are clear about what the client wants to get out of the experience. They must know that you will not be making decisions for them. Corporate clients can be used to consultants; people who will interpret their problems and then sell them a solution.

The great thing about LEGO Serious Play is that it completely subverts that process, but be prepared to address the gap in expectations that this creates.

Before you start, make sure you have a complete mutual understanding of the objectives and you will save yourself a rather painful workshop experience.

Kristina Nyzell

🐦 @disruptiveplay

Specialties:
Strategy & Innovation
Stealth Learning
Dialogue Partner

Play. With LEGO® Serious Play®

The same four things that I enjoyed doing as a child, I still enjoy now. I enjoy playing sports, playing music, using creative material to build something to solve problems and create communities with which I share my passions and joys in life.

The difference between children's play and Serious Play® can be boiled down to a few things: the type of questions we ask ourselves, the size, scope, risk and impact of the game as well as the complexity of the rules of the game itself. Ceteris Paribus (all other things being equal). The game process itself remains the same regardless of what kind of play we do.

There are many types of play, including Tool Play (where we learn to master the brick and the building system), Imaginary and Metaphorical Play (where we imagine the brick to be something other than a brick and use metaphors to put words to what is not yet fully understood or known to us), Rule Play and Role Play (where we begin to use the brick and the building system together with someone else and take turns in playing and learning from each other) and Collaborative Group Play (where the brick is

used within a community to co-create, collaborate and co-innovate to solve sticky problems).

There is so much scope to play, so my advice to people working with LEGO Serious Play is:

1. Build your own personal community of trainers, coaches, mentors, sparring partners, client ambassadors, former workshop participants, critics and workshop collaborators. Work together to create workshops that have an impact and that help to solve the challenges humanity is currently facing. Think big and think outside the box. LEGO Serious Play is a clever tool that has the power to unlock system level challenges.

2. Collaborate, co-create and co-innovate to grow sales opportunities, co-develop proposals and co-deliver LEGO Serious Play programs. Share the rewards, reflect on what went well and not so well and continuously learn and share learning with your trusted community. Don't be afraid to ask for help.

3. Grow the methodology by tinkering with it. Combine and recombine it with other game-based learning methodologies and academic disciplines. Don't be afraid to experiment, for you may have the idea that takes the whole system to the next level!

For me, the spirit of LEGO Serious Play is community, collaboration and play.

Other Practical Tips

How to manage time

Facilitate the people, not the process

Meeting and workshop facilitation is not about driving a process. For a book that has dedicated many pages to describing and narrating plans it might seem like a planned process is primary.

In fact, skilled facilitation is all about **facilitating the people**, not the process.

Facilitation notes and workshop plans should be used as a guide, rather than a fixed map. Good facilitators prepare plans, and are prepared to abandon or change the plan in-the-moment if it is no longer meeting the needs of the group in that moment.

Use facilitation notes as a guide

Sometimes some things you expect to be short take longer, sometimes longer planned activities are completed remarkably quickly.

We often write the real start and finish time on a paper print out of the facilitation notes and adjust timings as workshops proceed to ensure we don't suddenly arrive at the end of the workshop with only half the plan completed. You'll lose and gain some time as the workshop unfolds.

Cut the waffle

'Waffle.' Verb. To talk or write a lot without giving any useful information or any clear answers.

It's easy to lose time due to waffle, especially waffle that is off topic. As facilitators are not involved in the content, it is easier for them to pay attention to drifting topics and ask the individual or group if this is the time to be dealing with that off topic issue.

Sometimes some people can take a long time to make a simple point (or no point at all), so we sometimes use sticky notes or gridcards to ask people to summarise ideas. With a marker or fat pen you can only get 20 words on a card. Ask people to use the 'one gridcard rule.

PROCESS

THE ONE GRIDCARD RULE

YOU CAN ONLY READ OUT THE WORDS THAT ARE WRITTEN ON YOUR CARD TO EXPLAIN CLEARLY WHAT YOU MEAN.

When participants can only read out the words on the cards it is easy to hear the key ideas, but briefly!

Learn from our mistakes

So far in this book we've already covered some mistakes we've made (see poor clarity of objectives (page 69), and poor question design (page 68).

It's interesting to note that our book partners also highlighted these risks. Eli de Friend's third tip was to establish the real objectives, and Oliver Knapman paid the price of not having clear objectives with his client.

As Part 2 of this book is all about trying to establish clear objectives, it could be worth another read.

There are two final mistakes we'd like to share so you don't have to learn the hard way:

Rooms that are too small

Small, hot and cramped rooms make people hot and bothered. Sean made this mistake once and the participants were revolting.

Well not quite that bad, but as Winston Churchill, the British politician said in a speech in the House of Commons on October 28, 1944,

"We shape our buildings, and afterwards, they shape us."

Pay attention to the room or space that you intend to work in before your workshop begins.

Insufficient set up time

You want a calm and collected mind at the outset of a workshop, so give yourself more time than you think you need to set a workshop up. The worst that will happen is you'll have an extra 15 minutes to be calm and collected.

The bricks - how store them

If you don't have a huge pile of bricks to deal with, it might seem odd to be reading about something as basic as storing bricks. Once you have a growing set, however, you might find yourself vexing over the brick storage question.

Firstly we are sure there is no 'right' way. You'll find a solution that works for you. There do, however, seem to be two ends of the storage philosophy, from:

One big pile <<<>>> Neatly ordered and stored

One big pile

A LEGO Serious Play Facilitator friend of ours embraces the 'one big pile' idea. Jane has a big wheelie case that contains all her bricks, plus a few random objects.

Depending on the workshop setting she makes one big pile or several small piles of which ever bricks randomly appear.

The benefit of this approach is not needing to spend time sorting bricks and as Jane says, life is random, so a random distribution of bricks is no bad thing

Let there be order

For smaller workshops Sean uses the one big pile approach and selects bricks from his big brick box (page 83).

For multi-day workshops at Build Levels 2: Shared Models and Build Level 3: System Models it can be helpful to have an ordered approach.

Build levels 2 and 3 use specific bricks for specific purposes: Baseplates for building shared models, flags for identification of priorities and special rigid and flexible connections to build system models. It's best to keep those separate.

If someone is looking for a key, a magnifying glass, a rocket pod, money, a diamond, or a shark to tell the story they have in mind

It's easier to locate these bricks if they are compartmentalised, not just hopefully in the pile somewhere.

The plastic trays that come with the Landscape and Identity Kits and Connections Kits are not great for travel. The clip close trays shown on page 231 (with lids removed) make transport of organised bricks very easy.

Another good tip is to buy a good quality, large wheelie bag!

Serious LEGO® Movies

The visual nature of LEGO® is one its strengths. People are better able to remember ideas that have been communicated with models than ideas shared verbally only.

As you have seen in part 5, the models can be used on posters and other assets to keep the ideas alive after the workshop.

Video is another way to remember what was built and what the models meant.

When you video each story and project it on to a big screen, the whole room can see the ideas.

This is helpful in larger meetings or workshops to help share ideas, either to a larger group or from one table to another table. If you also record these videos you have the key ideas on film forever more.

WebCam or WiFi

A technically easy solution is to use an external USB webcam with a 10m extension cable plugged into a laptop that is connected to a projector.

Another option is to connect a mobile phone to a wireless network via an Apple TV that is connected to the projector.

This has the advantage of less cables. The photo on page 233 shows this set-up.

In both options there is a skill required in operating the camera to make sure the camera doesn't shake, that you record the right part of the model, and that the picture is sharp and the audio clear.

Unskilled camera operators create shaky videos that make people feel ill when they watch the screen and the video is not so usable afterwards.

You also need to ask everyone in the room to be quiet so you can record good quality audio.

If you upload videos to YouTube afterwards you can share them with workshop participants via a private link, and YouTube can remove camera shake and enhance lighting for you if the videos were not as good as you hoped for.

If you plan to record videos, allow at least another 20 minutes for set up and take many kinds of connectors and cables with you to cover all options. Note some wi-fi networks don't like video transmission. For that reason we now take our own wi-fi hub.

See example videos

We have put a selection of videos taken from workshops at: https://www.serious.global/videos/

Part 7

Becoming a virtuoso practitioner

OR WHY THE ALTERNATIVE SUBTITLE IS "WITH CONSCIOUS INCOMPETENCE"

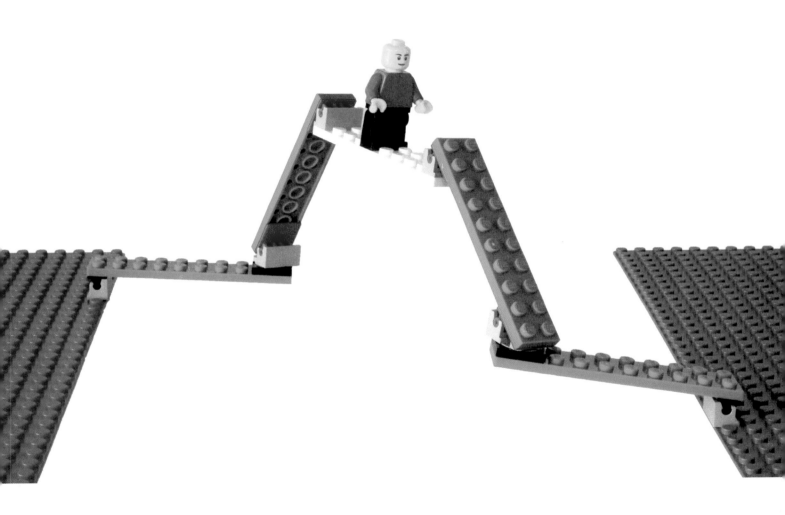

Imagine you want to abseil. You could read a "how-to" book about that.

Reading this book however wouldn't make you able to abseil safely or competently.

To really understand how to abseil you'd need a helping hand from a wise teacher who knows how to tie knots and who can guide you in real world practice.

Some 'hands-on' skills are best acquired by 'hands-on' doing.

Part 7: Becoming a virtuoso practitioner

The objective of this chapter is to outline three paths to becoming a skilled facilitator.

Some skills can only be mastered through doing. So called 'experiential knowledge' is the only way to learn how to competently perform some hands-on things in practice. How-to books like this one offer 'propositional knowledge.' You could read as many books as you like about **how to drive a car, perform CPR (cardiopulmonary resuscitation; 'the kiss of life') or abseil**, but this alone would not make you able to do these things safely or competently without real world practice and help from a wise teacher.

'Propositional knowledge,' which is the kind of knowledge you get from reading a book, can at best make aware practitioners consciously incompetent.

This book has an alternative subtitle, **"with conscious incompetence"** because to become a competent LEGO® Serious Play® Facilitator, or even a virtuoso facilitator, you'll need to learn by doing.

We suggest that readers who have not experienced LEGO Serious Play might have been at Stage 1 of the Competence Matrix as they began reading this book.

Most people who have read the whole book attentively might now be at Stage 2 (some readers, already skilled in facilitating hands on processes might feel they are now at Stage 3).

User testing of early drafts of this book suggested that reading alone was not enough to skilfully facilitate (get to Stage 3) and there maybe some facilitators, including our teachers, who might think it's folly to produce a 'how-to' book to try and teach such a hands-on process.

We had two objectives in writing this book: to enable you to **understand** how to facilitate LEGO Serious Play based meetings and workshops, with a deeper purpose **to help legitimise a brilliant and powerful method**.

Explaining how things work makes some people interested to learn more. That is what we hope this book has done. We hope it has helped you understand enough that you'd be interested to want to learn more.

And we hope that by explaining the LEGO Serious Play process it has gone some way to legitimising what we know to be a brilliant and powerful method.

With luck, we might have made some progress towards achieving the two objectives in your mind

Stage 1

UNCONSCIOUS INCOMPETENCE

You're unaware of the skill and your lack of proficiency

Stage 2

CONSCIOUS INCOMPETENCE

You're aware of the skill and your lack of proficiency

Stage 4

UNCONSCIOUS COMPETENCE

Performing the skill becomes automatic

Stage 3

CONSCIOUS COMPETENCE

You can use the skill but only with effort

Three practise paths

There are three obvious routes to developing your LEGO Serious Play skills.

1. Practise the ideas alone.

2. Experience the process with a trained facilitator.

3. Participate in a training program.

You might find a combination of these paths to be the best way to develop your skills.

1. Practise the ideas alone

This book has been written with the intention of enabling you to develop your Build Level 1: Individual Model Building skills alone.

We encourage you to find, or create a low-risk and friendly environment to

- practise a goal setting meeting.

- try a Skills Build workshop.

Before then setting up a safe space to explore a topic that is important to your group or organisation.

You might buy some bricks and try some of the simpler exercises and see how you get on.

Learn from your practise

With any test session, including one-to-ones ensure you evaluate your performance.

Be wise

You would indeed be wise to include a learning review of some kind after each of your practise sessions.

This will be a chance for you to workout what went well, but more importantly get some feedback on what could have gone better.

Make it OK for people to be honest in their feedback. In groups, spoken feedback tends to norm to what others have already said, which limits the range of useful feedback. You might consider putting the questions opposite on a feedback sheet to get BRIEF written answers.

2. Experience the process with a trained facilitator

A great way to get experiential learning is by being a participant in a workshop run by a trained LEGO Serious Play Facilitator.

You can both experience some of the ideas in this book (no doubt with sightly different twists and emphasises) and observe a facilitator in action.

If you live in a country or city where LEGO Serious Play MeetUps happen it's a great way to learn more.

Questions you might ask after your first meeting or workshop might include:

On a scale 1 to 5 (5 being high) how would you rate the workshop?

What needed to happen to be a 5?

What, if anything, was unclear or confusing?

If we did the workshop/session again, what small thing would you change to make it (even) better?

What could I have done better?

How effective was the session in achieving the objectives?

Where (if anywhere) did I look like I was struggling (in my facilitation)?

What strengths did you experience using LEGO® Serious Play®?

What weaknesses did you experience using LEGO® Serious Play®?

Is there anything else you'd like to tell me?

Sometimes you'll get better feedback if it's written, but don't leave it until later. If you plan to get feedback, allow 5 minutes at the end of the allotted time.

LEGO® Serious Play® Meetups

'MeetUp is an online social networking portal that facilitates offline group meetings in various localities around the world. MeetUp allows members to find and join groups unified by a common interest.'[8]

We founded the LEGO Serious Play MeetUps in London in 2014 and encouraged our peers to set up LEGO Serious Play MeetUps in other cities and countries.

There are now over 40 all over the world.

https://www.meetup.com

Be aware that there is no quality control; we know of some LEGO Serious Play MeetUp's that are run by people who have not undertaken LEGO Serious Play training courses. LEGO® MeetUps are not meant to be sales pitches, so best to read reviews of MeetUps before signing up.

[8.] From Wikipedia

A happy Justin during a Serious Work Level 1:
Individual Model Building Training Workshop

Playcamps and conferences

Another way to experience LEGO Serious Play is at conferences. The Agile Community has picked up on LEGO Serious Play so you might find opportunities to attend a session www.playcamp.net.

If you are organising the kind of conference where people exchange practices, you could consider inviting a LEGO Serious Play Facilitator to run a session. If you live in the same city as the contributors of this book, consider asking one of us to come and help.

3. LEGO Serious Play Training

Training programmes are a recommended route to learn more, especially for professionals who spend their lives helping people work together.

If you are considering taking a LEGO Serious Play Facilitator Training Course, ask: What kind of meetings, workshops, projects or applications do I plan to facilitate?.

Assess what you plan to facilitate

A good way to assess the kind of training you need is to consider the applications or kinds of meeting or workshop you'll lead or facilitate. There is a table on the pages that follow that might help you assess the kinds of skills you might need for different applications.

Learn the skills you need

Facilitation of Build Level 1: Individual Models enables you to enhance communication on any issue, unlock learning, set goals, offer feedback, mentor or coach. You can facilitate many kinds of meetings with just this Build Level.

However, if you need to help teams create common understanding on shared concerns like team vision, you'll need to understand how to facilitate Build Level 2: Shared Model Building.

Remember this book has focused on Build Level 1 facilitation techniques. This is the foundation of all LEGO Serious Play meetings and workshops, and you can do a lot with Level One.

There are longer and shorter training offers available on the market from which you can choose the most appropriate.

We advise that it's worth being clear about what you think you might want to facilitate before deciding on what kind of training course might serve your needs.

Once you are clear about what type of meeting you want to facilitate, head to www.serious.global/learn to find information on training options.

Considering training? Ask, what do I want to facilitate?

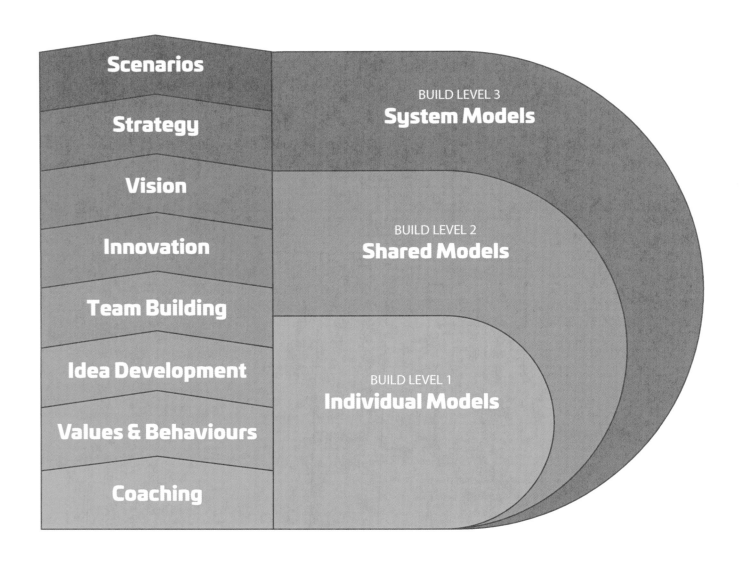

Scenarios

Strategy

Vision

Innovation

Team Building

Idea Development

Values & Behaviours

Coaching

BUILD LEVEL 3
System Models

BUILD LEVEL 2
Shared Models

BUILD LEVEL 1
Individual Models

... then what level of LEGO® Serious Play® skills do I need?

The kinds of skills you'll need for different jobs or responsibilities.

LEGO® Serious Play® **Advanced Skills**

Build Level 3: System Modelling

Create and use scenarios to explore dynamic systems and 'real time strategy.' Understand, change and develop simple guiding principles. Model, analyse and redesign processes and systems. Understand how external and internal factors influence goals.

LEGO® Serious Play® **Intermediate Skills**

Build Level 2: Shared Model Building

Create common understanding on shared concerns. Develop shared vision and goals, shared direction, plans, strategies and mental models. Build teams, design new services and innovate. Use LEGO® Serious Play® to create deeper agreement processes.

LEGO® Serious Play® **Core Foundation Skills**

Build Level 1: Individual Model Building

Enhance communication on any issue. Develop ideas and build trust. Manage staff, set goals and offer feedback. Mentor and coach. Explore and agree values and behaviours. Unlock both individual and group communication and learning on any topic.

Learn more:

serious.global/learn

Read More

Books

At time of going to press with this book there is only one other book written about LEGO Serious Play.

Building Better Business Using the LEGO Serious Play Method, published by Wiley, sets out the history, territory and science that underpins LEGO Serious Play, and provides some brief case studies. If you would like to know more about the history, development, science and context of LEGO Serious Play, it's a good read.

Case studies

There are a growing number of case studies of LEGO Serious Play in use in a wide range of applications on the ProMeet website:

http://www.meeting-facilitation.co.uk/lego-serious-play-london/

Join an online community

A great place to go to read case studies, post questions, and learn more is SeriousPlayPro. Whilst there are a couple of other online communities for LEGO Serious Play, the best and most active is https://seriousplaypro.com.

🐦 @SeriousPlayPro

So much more

It has been a fun experience writing and designing this book, and yet it only really scratches the surface of the LEGO Serious Play world.

There is so much more that has been unsaid in this book. LEGO Serious Play has incredible power at the higher build levels and as the method grows and combines with other brilliant processes, its potential as a tool expands.

We hope this book helps contribute to the inevitable evolution and development of LEGO Serious Play practice and pedagogy.

Connect

If you'd like to connect, you can find us here:

Serious Work
🐦 @SeriousWrk
Sean@Serious.Global

Sean Blair
🐦 @ProMeetings
🔗 https://uk.linkedin.com/in/sean-blair

Marko Rillo
🐦 @MarkoRillo
🔗 https://www.linkedin.com/in/markorillo

Final word

Thank you for reading this book. We hope you enjoyed it.

We started this book with a hypothetical foreword from the future. In our vision we sincerely hope to see that LEGO® Serious Play® will eventually become as common as a flip-chart and markers.

We hope to see LEGO Serious Play applied to businesses and schools, as well as taken up by coaches and counsellors. We also hope that it will become a tool used by a new generation of leaders; leaders who value participation and who preach and practice a facilitative mind-set.

We live in challenging times.

Humanity has not yet learnt how to live in peace with each other, or in harmony with the incredible planet Earth we are so very lucky to call home. One of the biggest underlying challenges is to truly and deeply understand each other and to change the way we perceive the complexities we face.

We think that humans have four type of knowledge.

First is the dominant mode of knowledge, which is with our thoughts and mind. Hey brain! You sure do think you rule the game.

Then there is knowledge from our bodies, such as feelings, intuition and wise hands.

Thirdly there is the knowledge from the heart that soars or aches with people we love.

Finally, there is knowledge of the spirit or soul.

LEGO Serious Play for its brilliance, appeals to knowledge of the brain and body. Knowledge of the heart and soul is more difficult to touch with a plastic cuboid.

Yet, combining LEGO Serious Play with deeper human-to-human interaction helps to create a dialogue and reveal insights into the kind of insight LEGO® system models can reveal. Insight that can touch our feelings and enrich our spirits - now that's a tantalizing prospect.

What if we could all become better and more participatory leaders and use the systems power of LEGO Serious Play to generate more meaningful, deeper and sustainable world-views and ideas?

Then we could indeed come to a situation where LEGO could turn into a serious tool that saved the world.

A fanciful vision?

Maybe, just maybe!

🐦 @seriouswrk